MARINE HUGONNIER

FILM AND VIDEO UMBRELLA
DUNDEE CONTEMPORARY ARTS

This publication is the first significant survey of the work of the artist Marine Hugonnier and acts as a companion publication to her solo exhibition at Dundee Contemporary Arts in Summer 2004. Alongside a number of large-scale photographic works, the show brought together two equally striking and impressive film pieces, *Ariana* and *The Last Tour*, that continue Hugonnier's long-standing fascination with images of landscape, as represented in visual art and cinema, and as reflected across a wider field of contemporary culture.

After the opening flourish of two emblematic, introductory works – a bouquet of flowers and a single frame of a film shot at night that resembles a piece of black film leader – the exhibition featured a series of haunting, frequently breathtaking landscapes. With their timeless seascapes and rugged mountain scenes, the photographic series *Towards Tomorrow (International Date Line, Alaska)* and *Mountains With No Name (Pandjshêr Valley, Afghanistan)* draw on a tradition of the Romantic sublime, an aura of grandeur and vastness, that is contrasted, in each of the pieces, with the desire to name, order and regulate the natural world. This theme is extended in the two film works, reaching rare heights of insight and sophistication. Here, too, at the heart of two intricate and compelling fictional narratives, is a set of equally evocative landscapes — landscapes with complex and resonant histories, landscapes weighted with increasing strategic implications,

landscapes embodying wider social and philosophical concerns. Evoking a feeling of awe, or instilling a spirit of contemplation, Hugonnier's vivid trail of images also stimulates thinking, about our contemporary relationship with nature, and our apparent need to fix it and frame it, to control it and contain it.

This book attempts to draw out some of the background to this remarkable body of work, and in this we are indebted to our three writers, Michael Newman, Jeremy Millar and Lynne Cooke. We are also grateful to Stuart Smith for his considerate and sensitive approach to the design of this publication. The book is the result of a close collaboration between Film and Video Umbrella and Dundee Contemporary Arts, following on from our organisations' involvement in the commissioning of *Ariana* and *The Last Tour* respectively. For support and assistance on each of these projects, we would like to thank Max Wigram at MW Projects, London, and also Juerg Judin at Galerie Judin, Zürich for his involvement in the production of *The Last Tour*. And finally, our thanks go to the artist herself for the undivided attention and commitment she brings to all of her work.

Steven Bode
Director
Film and Video Umbrella

Katrina M. Brown
Curator/Deputy Director
Dundee Contemporary Arts

Flower

1998/2000
Fresh flowers, spray paint for flowers, vase, water

'Flower' was first presented in 2000 at Galerie Chantal Crousel in Paris. The work comprises a list of flowers, which is reinterpreted each time it is shown, depending on the season, the location and the florist who arranges the bouquet. The flowers are changed every three to four days. The bouquet should not appear to be in full bloom, the flowers should always be crisp and fresh. Each flower is painted its own natural colour with special florists' spray-paint. The spray leaves a fine coat of paint on the flower. The colour of each flower is therefore very subtly enhanced. The bouquet illustrated here is the fourth version of this work, made by Jenny Fraser at Waow Studio for the exhibition at Dundee Contemporary Arts in June 2004.

List of flowers
7 branches of Elder
40 white roses
25 white peonies
10 Casablanca lilies
10 parrot tulips
15 white friesia

Spray paint   Oasis floral product, Art. 5101/yellow,
Art. 5104/white

Reproduction   300 dpi scan from original ektachrome printed
offset litho on Hello matt 170gsm

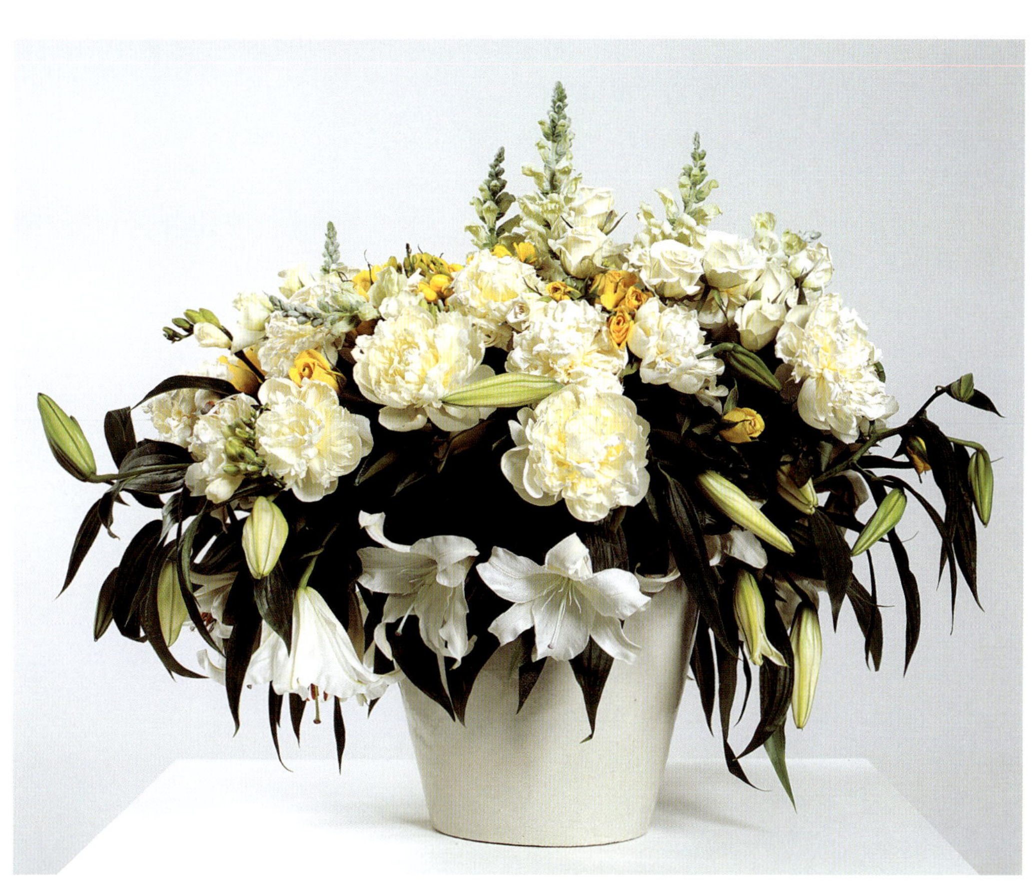

Leader (Oukaimeden, Morocco)

1996/2004
Lambda print mounted on aluminium
300 x 180 cm

'Leader' is one frame of a Super 16mm film shot at night in the
mountains of Oukaimeden, Morocco.

Shoot Oukaimeden, High Atlas, Morocco, February 1996
Camera Arriflex ST converted to super 16mm
Stock 7245/50 Asa
Lenses 25 mm, 50 mm Zeiss
Aspect ratio 1:85
Processed Cinedia, Paris
Print Grieger, Dusseldorf
Aluminium mount and frame Bliss, London/Darbyshire, London
Production Dundee Contemporary Arts

Reproduction 300 dpi scan from original frame printed offset
litho on Hello matt 170gsm

Towards Tomorrow (International Date Line, Alaska)

2001
6 lamdba prints mounted on aluminium
200x 130 cm
3 lamdba prints mounted on aluminium
160 x 120 cm
2 lambda prints mounted on aluminium
300x 180 cm

'Towards Tomorrow' is the result of a trip to the Bering Strait in
Alaska, USA, to photograph across the International Date Line into
Siberia. Due to its geographical position, Siberia is always 24 hours
ahead of Alaska. The photographs are therefore, in effect, pictures
of a future moment.

shoot Whales, Bering Strait, Alaska, Sept 2001
camera Linhof 8 x 10 Kardan GT
Stock 160 NC Portra Kodak
Lens 360 mm Schneider
Assistant Steve Schauer
Executive Producer Julie Gonssard
Processed Color Edge, New York/Metro, London
Print Glorious Productions, London/Grieger, Dusseldorf
Aluminium mount and frame Bliss, London/Darbyshire, London
Production MW Projects, London

Reproduction 300 dpi scan from original negatives printed offset
litho on Hello matt 170gsm

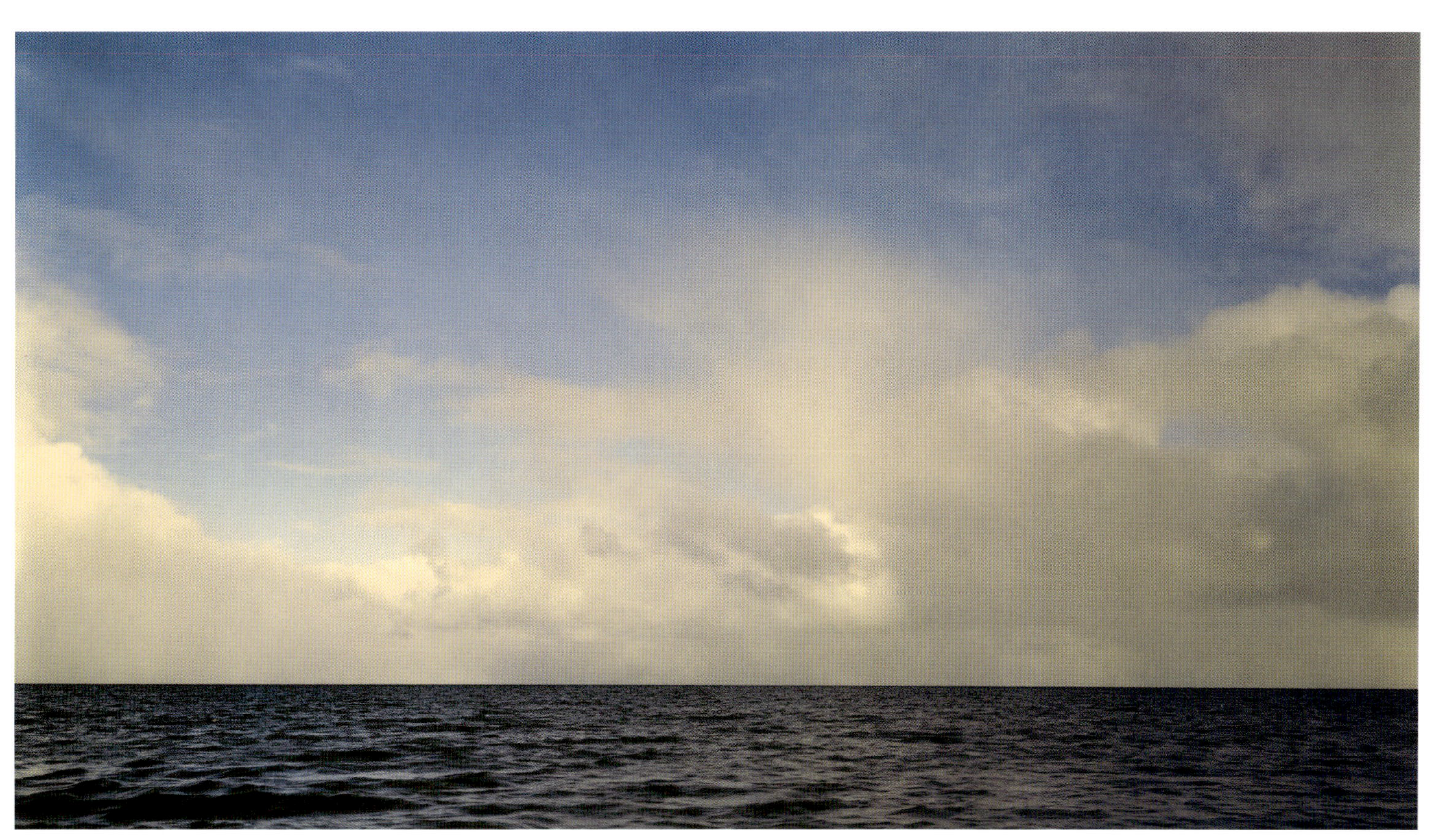

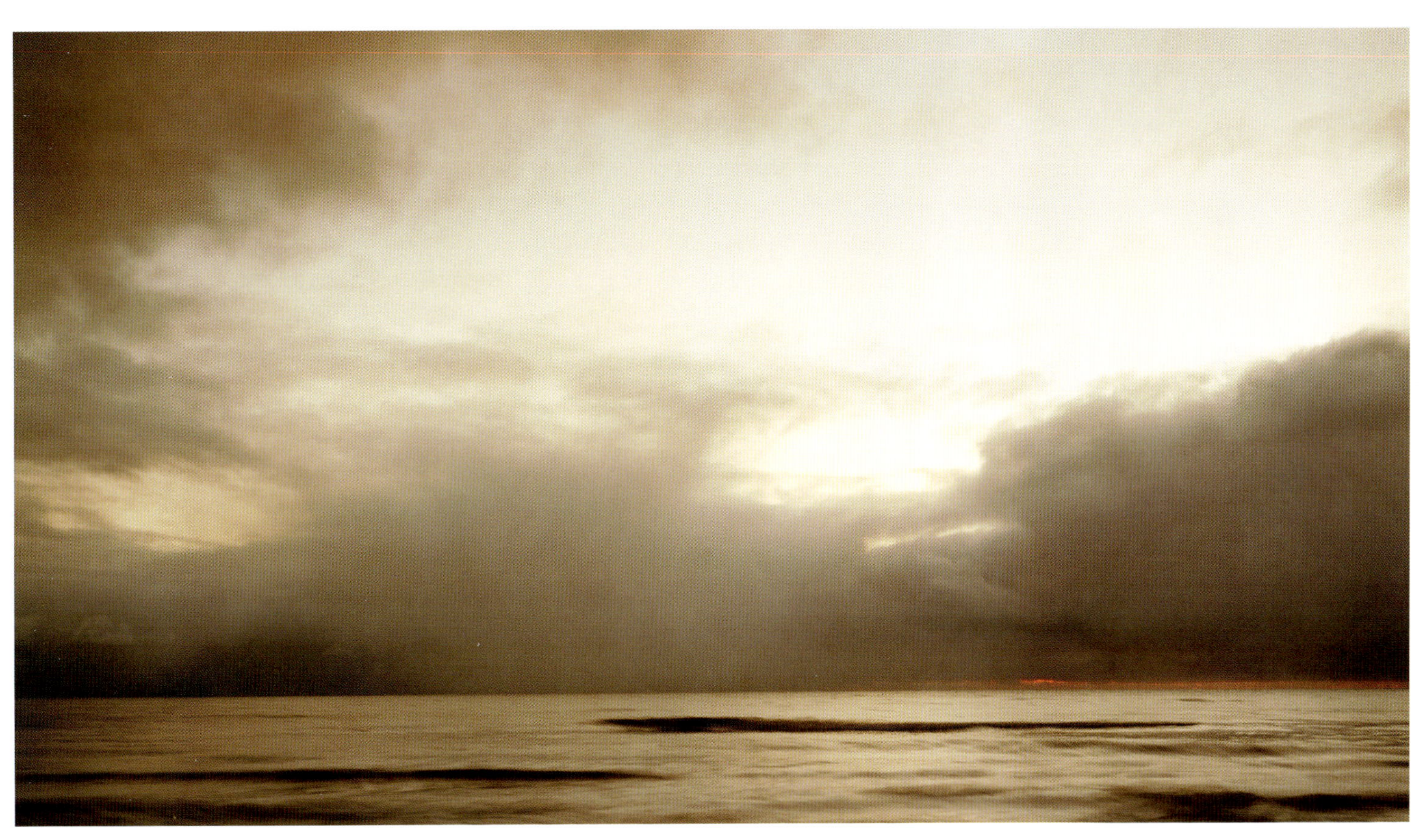

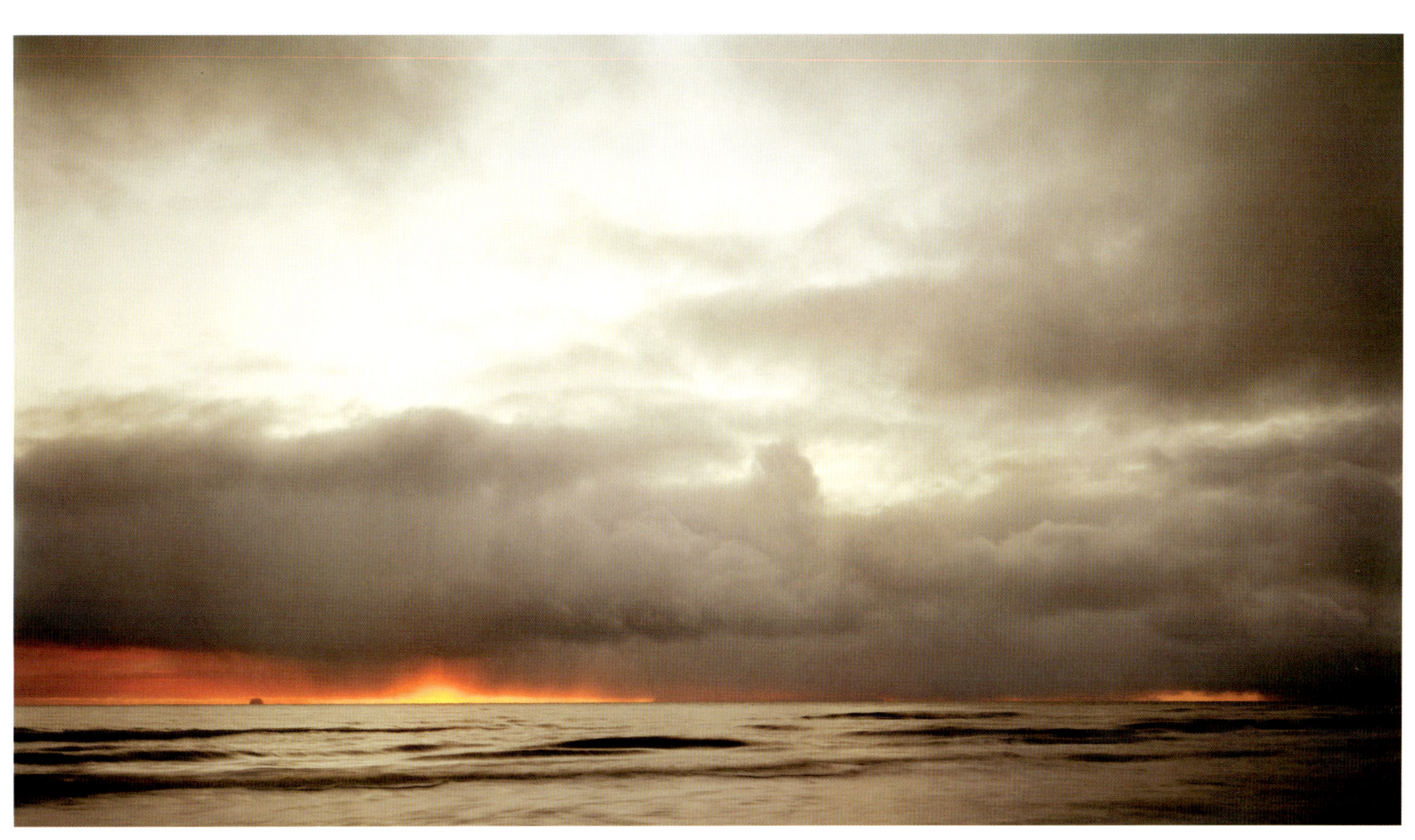

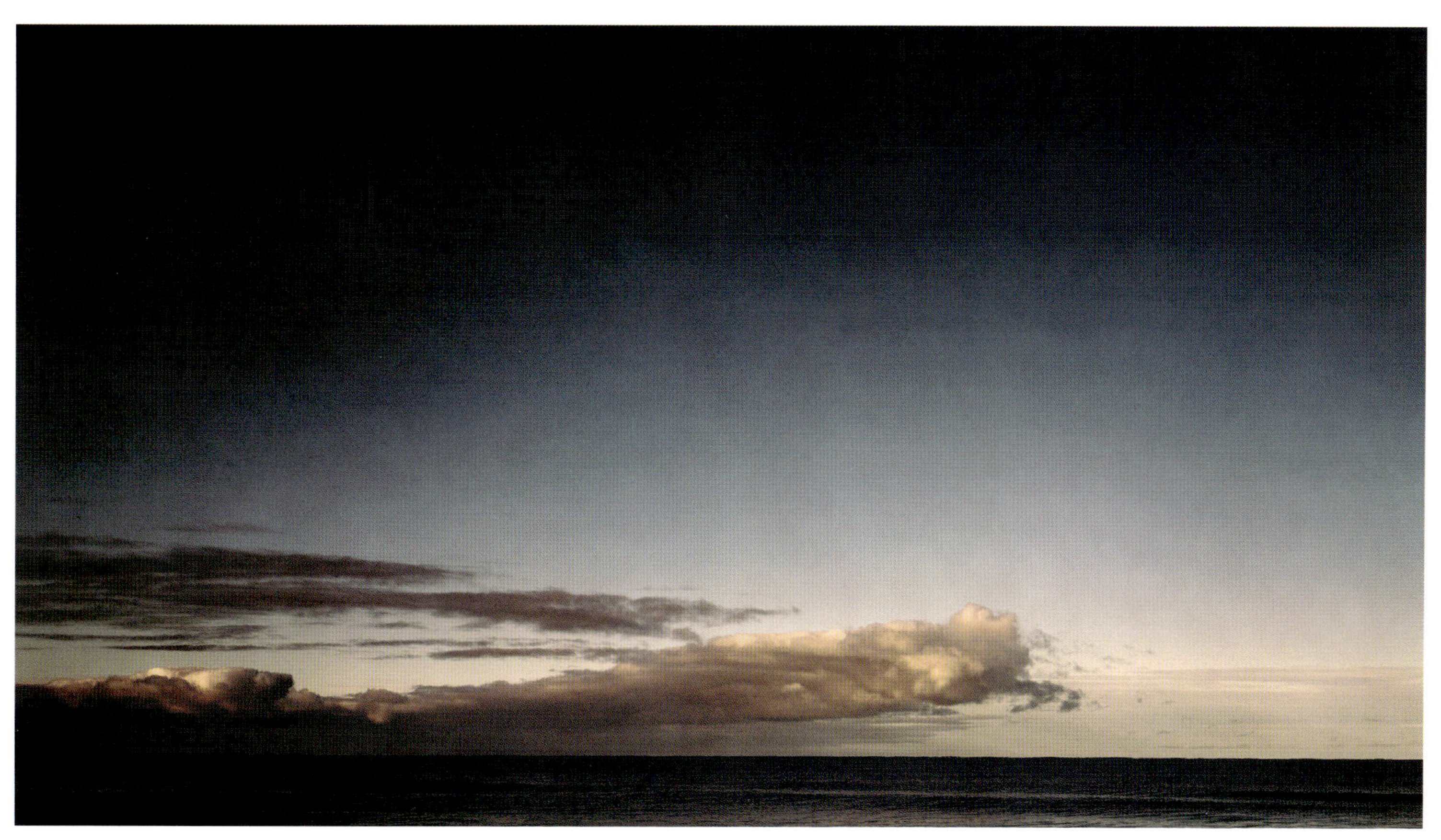

An image would

be missing.

Ariana

2003
Super 16mm film transferred onto DVD with sound.
Duration   18.36 minutes

'Ariana' tells the story of a film crew that sets out to visit the
Pandjshêr Valley in Northern Afghanistan. Described in classic
Persian poetry as a 'paradise garden', the impenetrable nature of
the valley and its lush, fertile landscape have set it apart from the
rest of the country and encouraged a history of independence and
resistance. The film considers how the specificities of a landscape
help to determine its history. As the crew is unable to film the valley
from a vantage point in the surrounding Hindu Kush mountains, the
film becomes the story of a failed project that prompts a process
of reflection about the 'panorama' as a form of strategic overview,
as a cinematic camera move, and about its origins as a pre-cinematic
mass entertainment.

Shoot   Pandjshêr Valley and Kabul, Afghanistan, August and
October 2002
Camera   ARRI SR3 Super 16mm
Stock   7245/50asa, 7246/250asa, 7289/500asa kodak
Lenses   9mm,12mm, 16mm, 25mm & 50mm Zeiss Primes, 10-100mm
Canon Zoom.
Aspect ratio   1:85
Director of Photography   Tom Townend
Editor   Ida Bregninge
Sound   Aurelien Bras
Executive Producers   Julie Gonssard/Marine Hugonnier
Processed   Éclair, Joinville
Graded   One Post, London
Post Production   Frontline Television, London
Produced by   MW Projects and Film and Video Umbrella in
association with Chisenhale Gallery, London
Supported by   The National Touring Programme of Arts Council,
England
Sponsored by   Marion and Guy Naggar, Alan Djanogly.

Reproduction   300 dpi scan from original telecinema printed offset
litho on Hello matt 170gsm

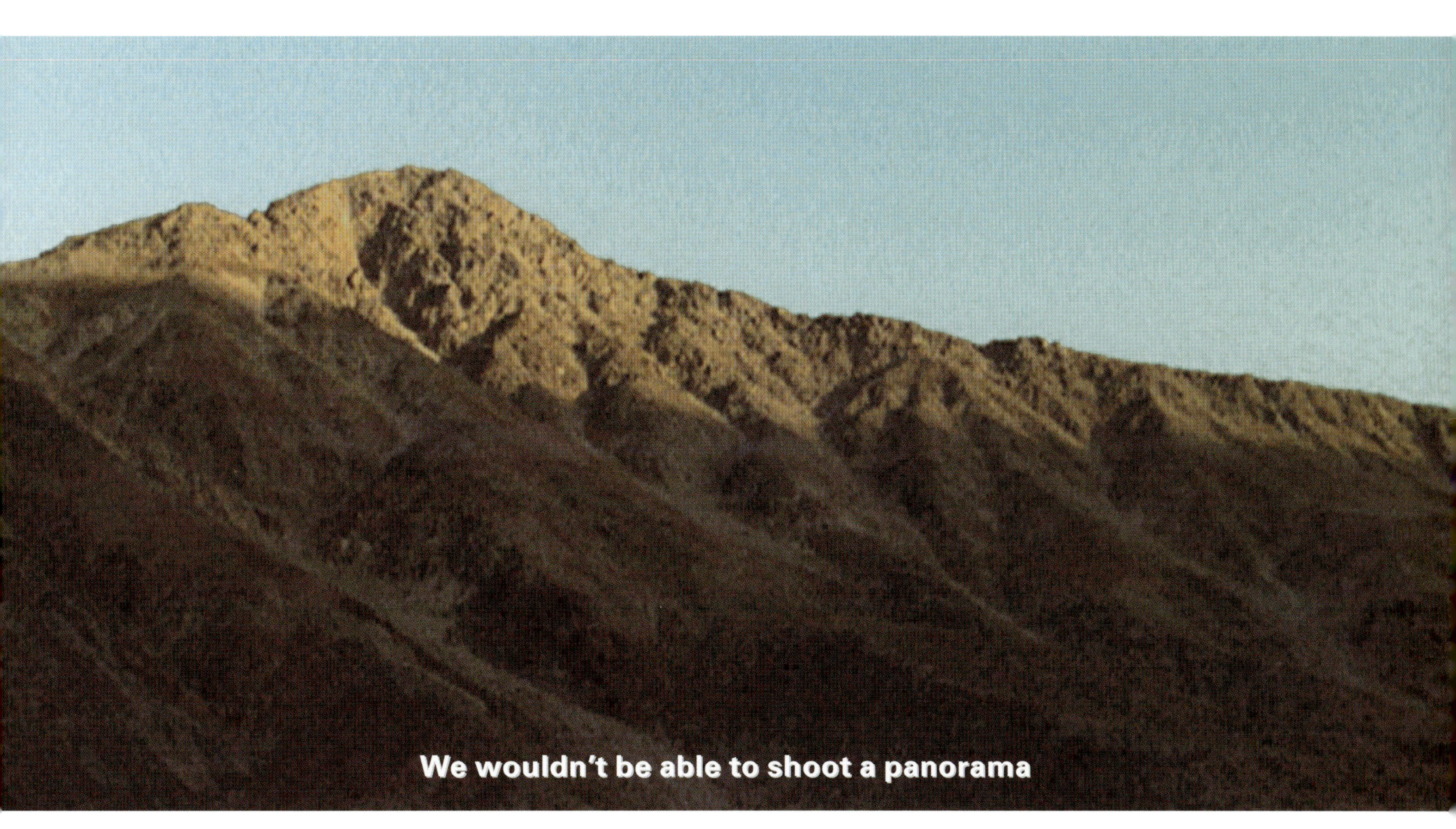
We wouldn't be able to shoot a panorama

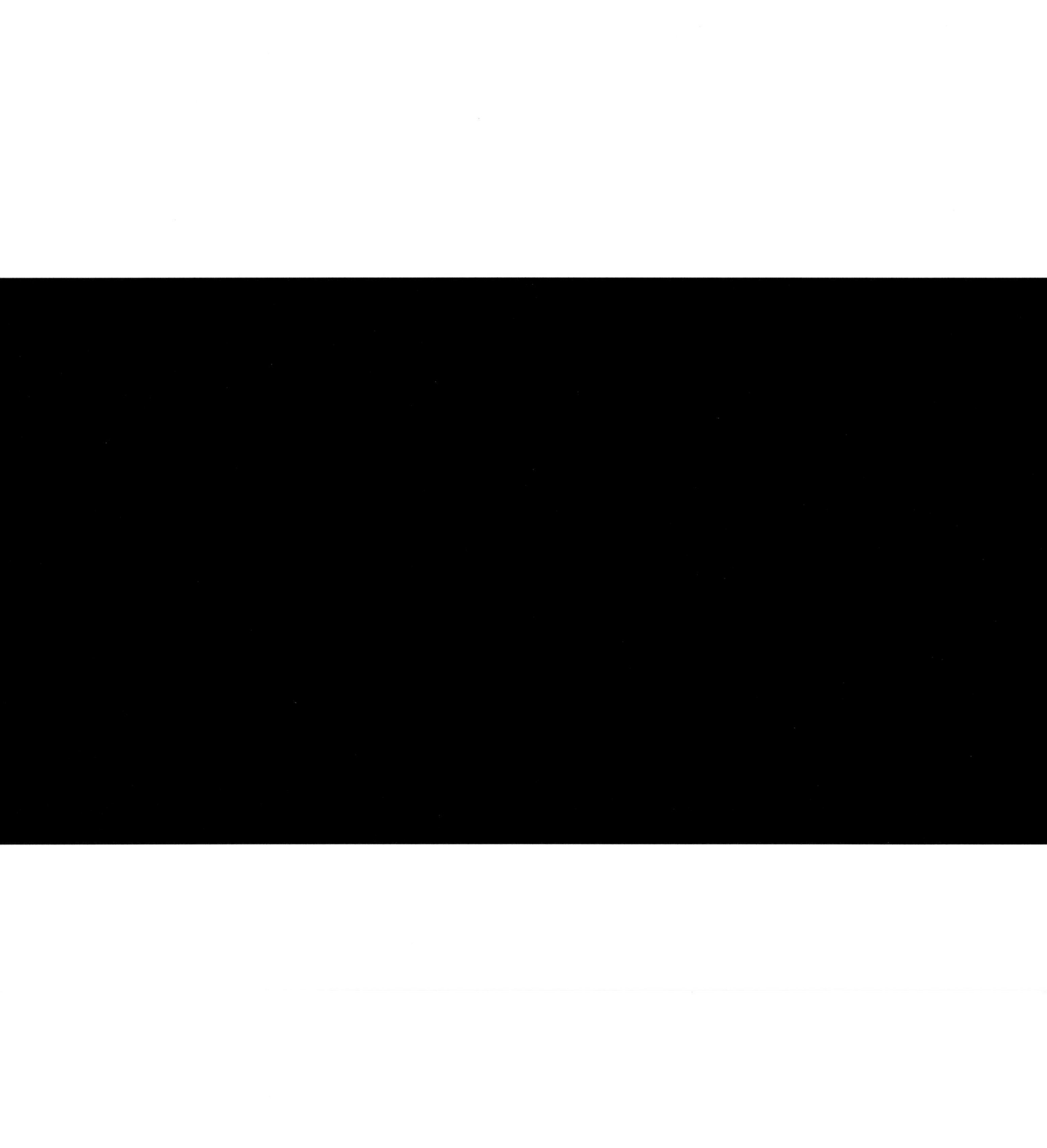

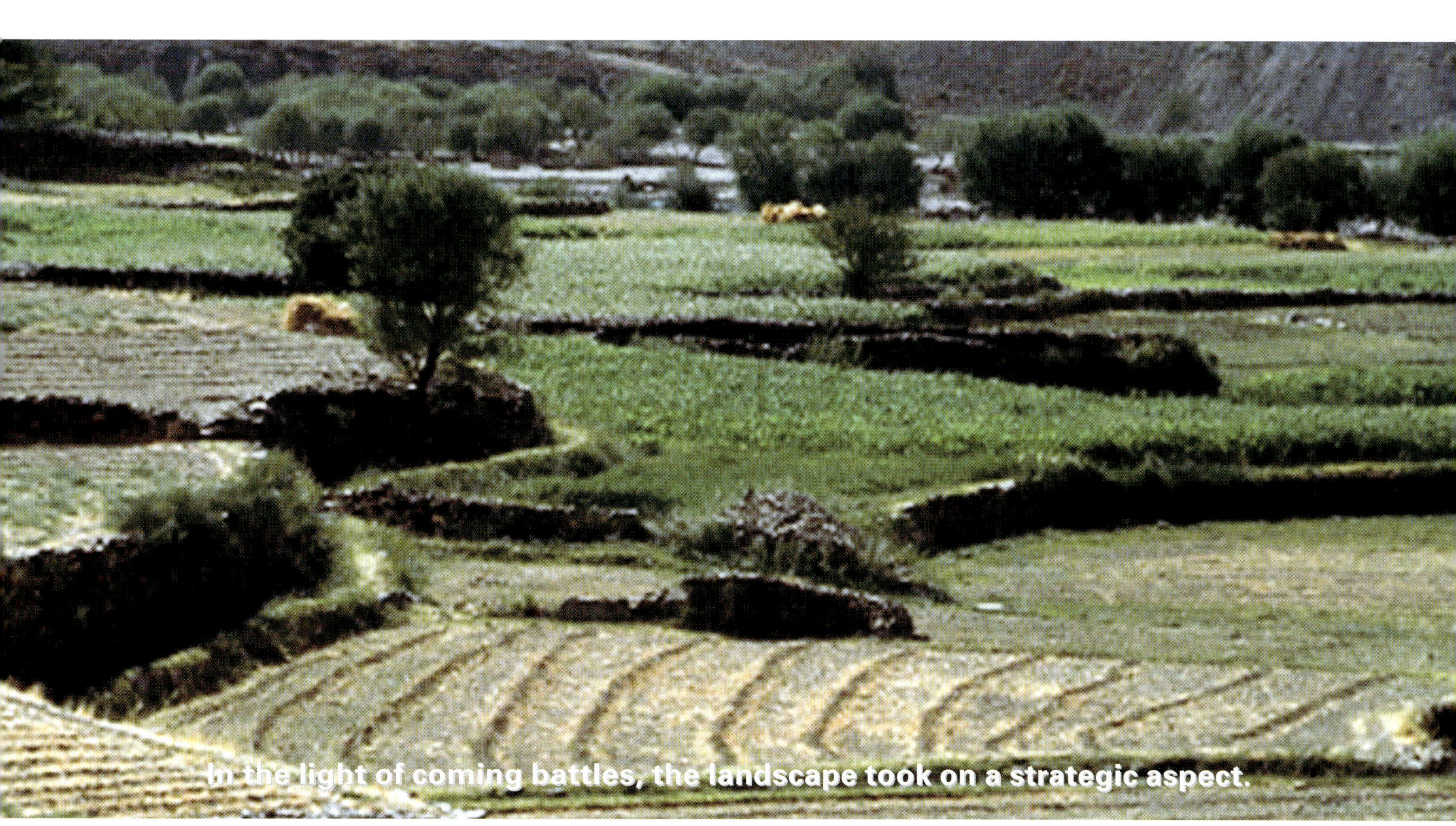
In the light of coming battles, the landscape took on a strategic aspect.

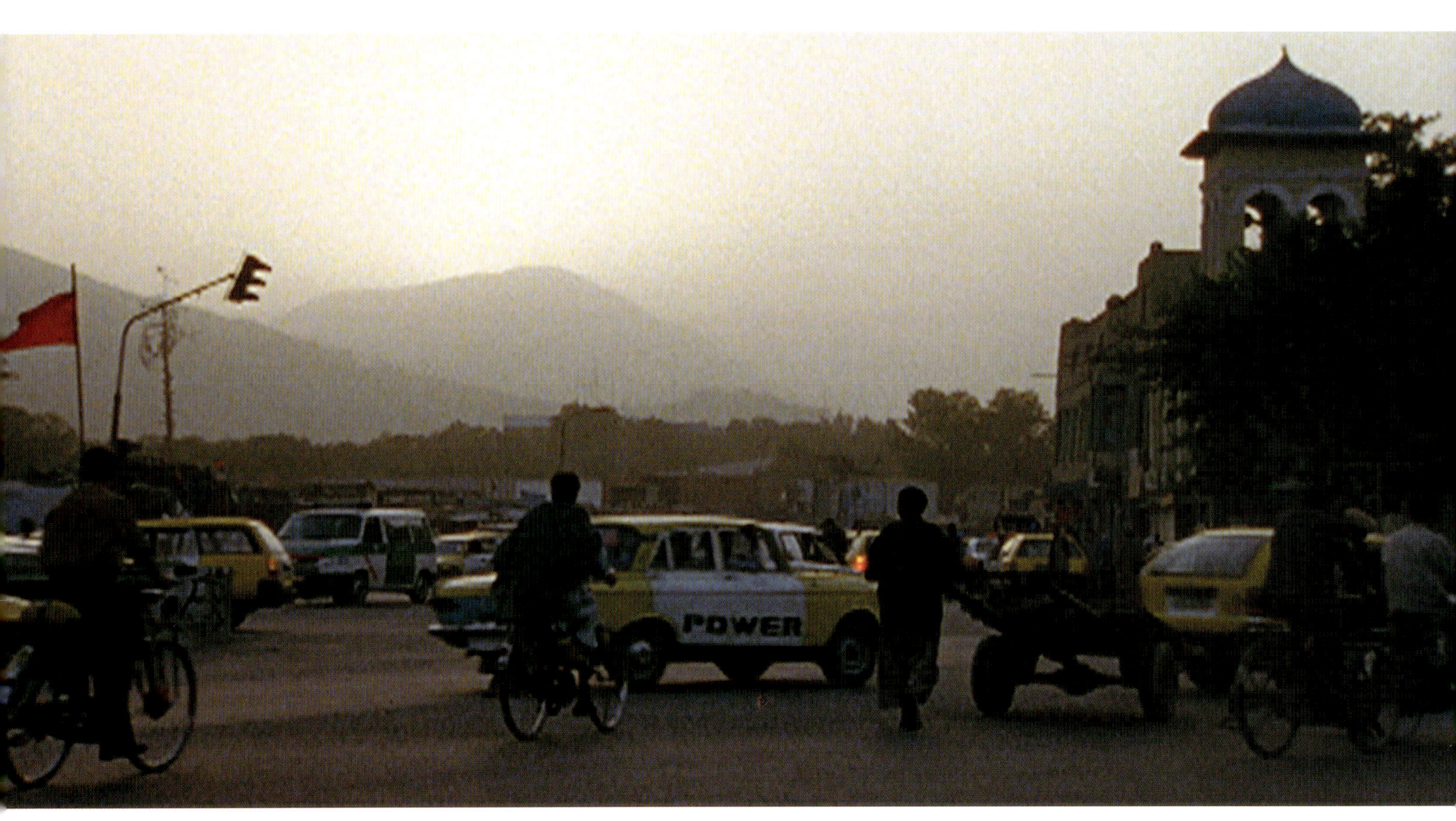

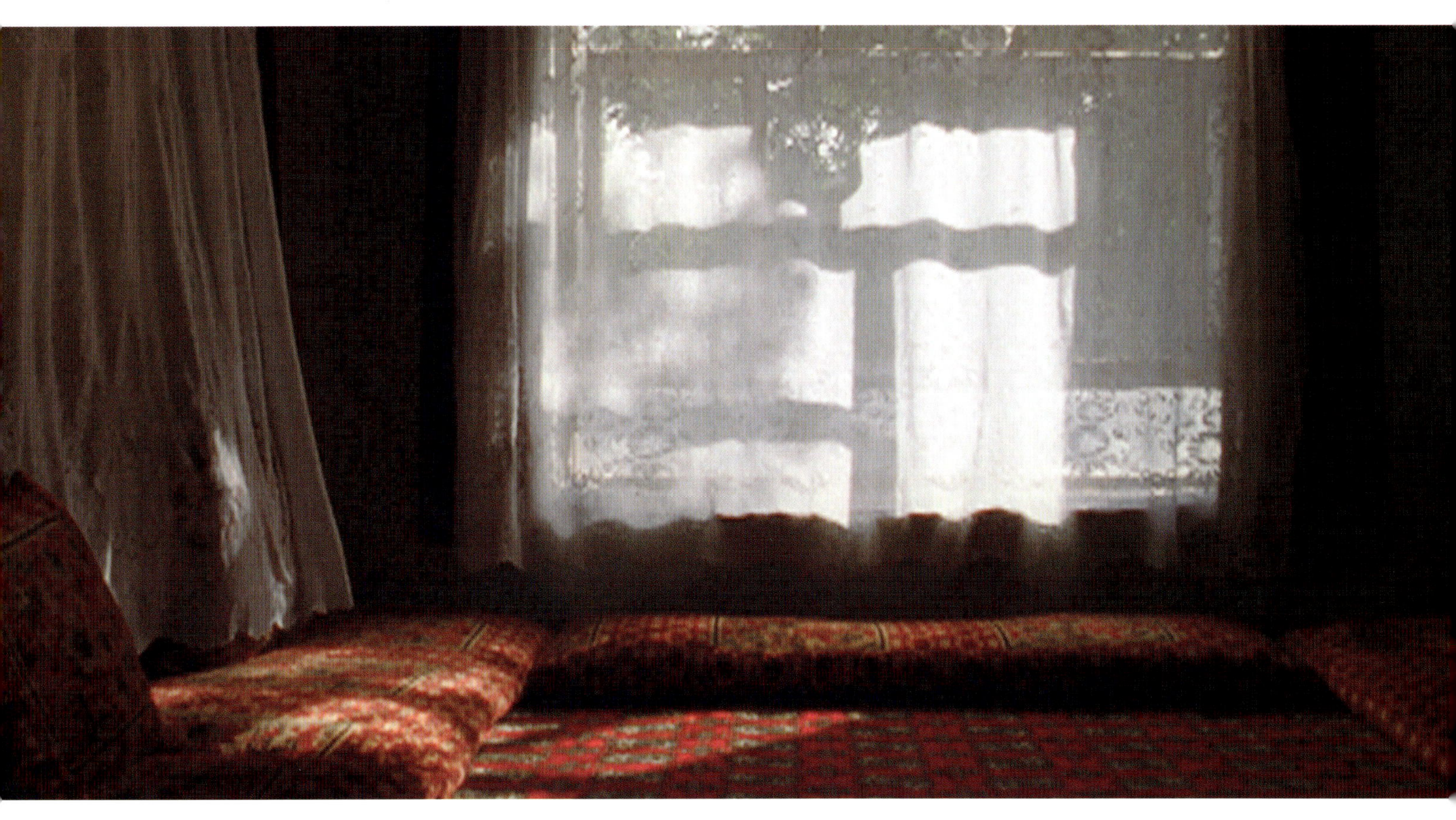

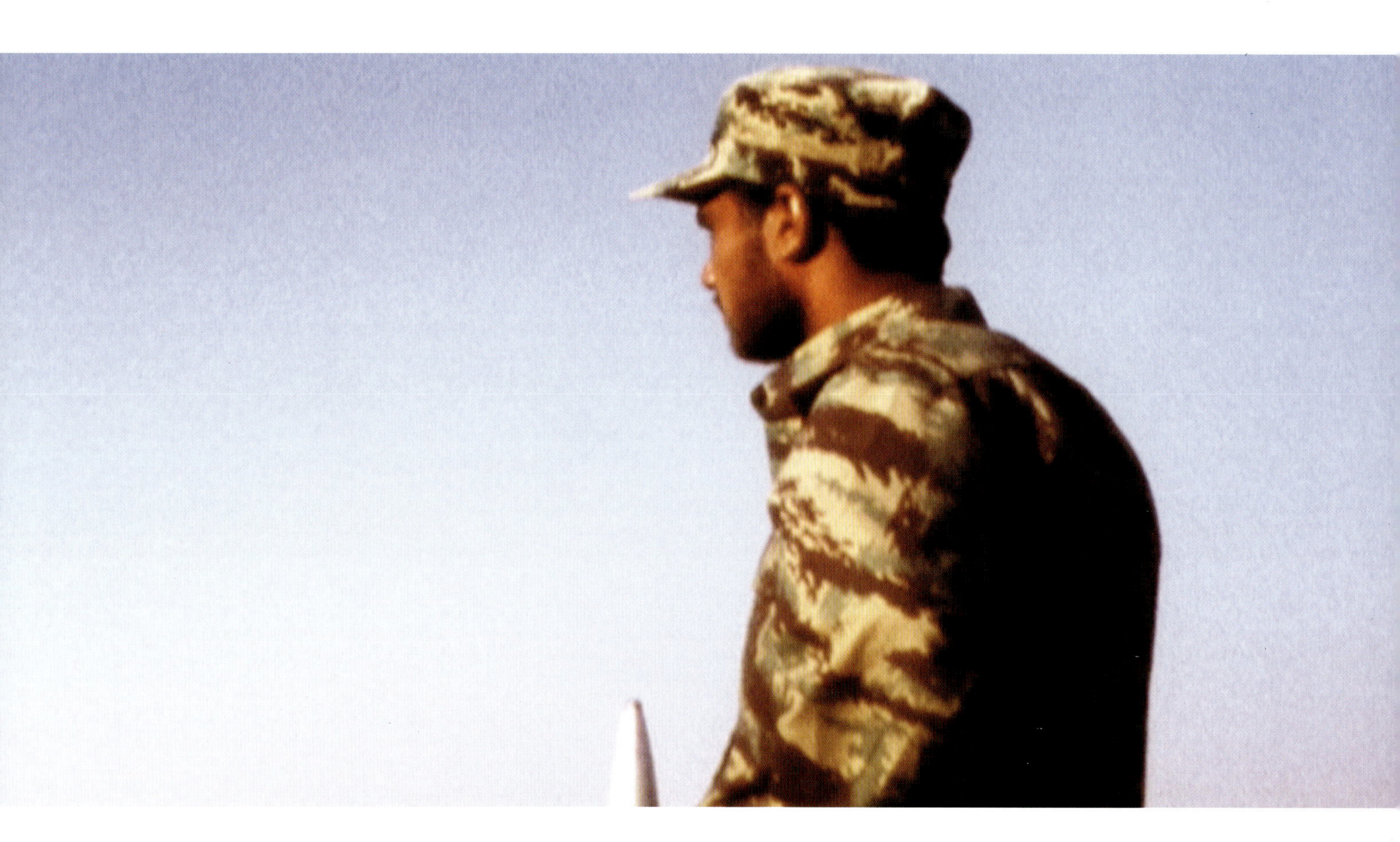

We gave up filming.

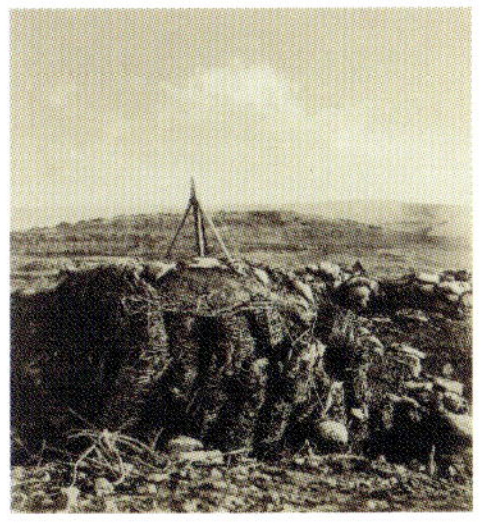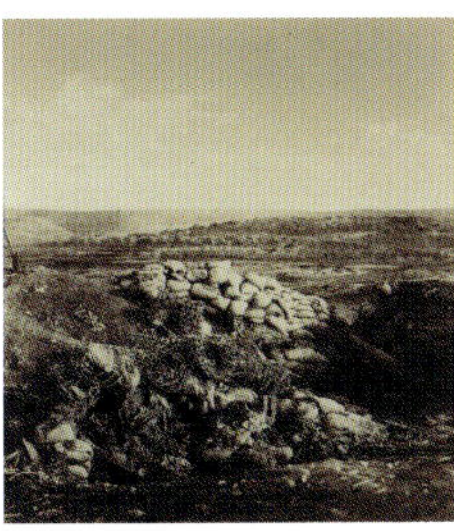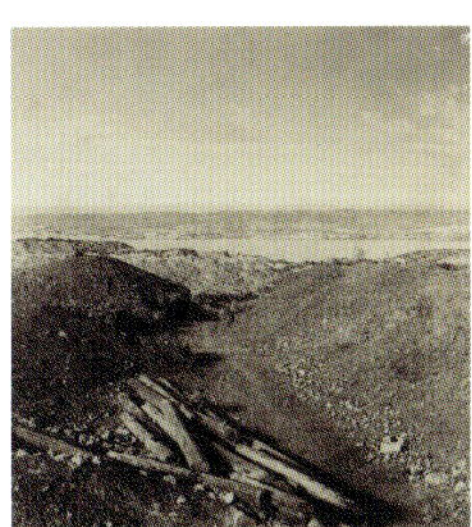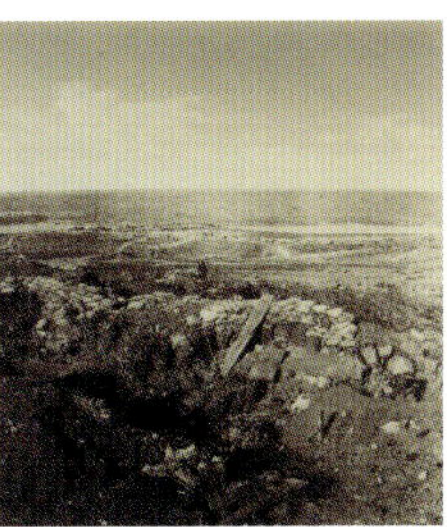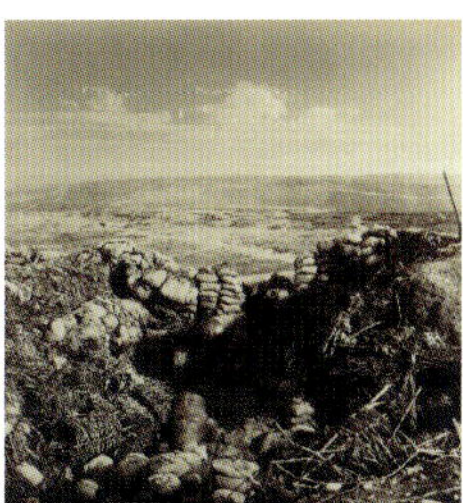

Jean-Charles Langlois, *Panorama de Sébastopol pris de la tour Malakoff*, 1855
© Patrice Schmidt/Musee D'Orsay

Just before launching the airstrikes, the U.S. Defense department purchased the rights to all available satellite images of Afghanistan and neighboring countries…The CEO of Space Imaging Inc. said, 'They are buying all the imagery available.' There is nothing left to see.[1]

The satellite image is the apotheosis of the overview, and the impetus for its development was the desire for military domination and control. It is no coincidence that in the 19th century a craze for balloons accompanied one for panoramas. Balloon and panorama were different but complementary: the former offered an overview of the landscape, the latter an immersive experience that replaced it; but both were in pursuit of control through a view that was as total as the technology of the time allowed. The military uses of the balloon are well known; less obvious are the military connections in the origins of the panorama. Just over 250 years ago the brothers Paul and Thomas Sandby travelled in the Highlands of Scotland, where the Jacobite Rebellion had been crushed in 1746, for the Military Survey, using a camera obscura to make accurate renditions of the terrain, including panoramic views. "Only detailed cartographic data," Olivier Grau writes, "could be used effectively to play through questions of tactics, field of fire, positions for advance and retreat, and the like…"[2] He goes on to describe how, after the first public exhibition of a panorama by Robert Barker in London in 1793, Paul Sandby, who must have been familiar with Barker's invention, went on to create a 'room of illusion' by covering the walls with a wild and romantic landscape, without framing elements.[3] Barker also had military affiliations: his studio in Edinburgh was the Guards Room of the castle of a high-ranking military officer, Lord Elcho, at Holyrood, and it was there that he made the first panorama, a 21-metre-long, 180-degree view of the city. "Thus, the inception of the panorama was characterised by a combination of media and military history."[4] True to its military origins, one of the most popular subjects for panoramas,

in addition to cityscapes and exotic foreign countries, was battles.

The Crimean War of 1853-56 was the first battleground to offer itself as a subject for photography. Since the long exposure times of early cameras meant that the fighting itself could not be captured, photographers often resorted instead to a study of the surrounding landscape, a landscape that was for the most part depicted as empty of people. Jean-Charles Langlois, a retired French colonel and a battle painter who was commissioned with Louis Mehedin to create a panorama of the siege of Sebastopol, took a panoramic series of photographs of Sebastopol from a tower surrounded by sandbagged fortifications, so the viewer is placed in the position of a soldier.[5] However, the ruined and disordered state of the defences suggests not a battle in progress or to come, but rather the deserted aftermath. In making his painted *Panorama of Sébastopol* (1856), Langlois used projections of photographs.[6] In 1862-63, Langlois prepared a painted panorama on the basis of topographical photographs of the 1859 Battle of Solferino between the French and the Austrians.[7] Concurrently, in the United States Civil War of 1861-65, photographers formed part of the topographical section of General Sherman's Union army, providing images to help draw up maps and plans.[8] Later, during the First World War this surveying function was supported by aerial photography.

The first shot in Marine Hugonnier's film *Ariana* is a view from an airplane window of a dry mountain range. Later there is a shot that is an extended pan of a location in the lush Pandjshêr Valley in Northern Afghanistan. We are told in the voice-over, as translated by the subtitles, "Neither of the two revolutionary utopias which had ruined the country had ever entered this place",[9] and it is suggested that this is because it is "protected by its mountains." What we are shown – the fertile valley, and later on boys swimming in the river – appears idyllic, as if in reference to traditional depictions of paradise, which doesn't exclude the possibility that this is an outsider's idealisation. The pan transforms this idyll into a strategic terrain. The voice-over says:

In the light of coming battles, the landscape took on a strategic aspect./Every contour of land, pass and gorge, every shadow of a rock, lookout and footpath, was seen as a potential shelter,/ a hiding place, or a line of approach to be hidden from enemy eyes./Each specific feature, hollow, mound and viewpoint was thought of as a zone to control, a forward position to hold, a place to fall back to.

And then the question is posed:

And if the best point of view was not accessible to us, was it because it was also a strategic point?

The mountains provide a potential vantage point for the pan, the name for a rotating shot (from the Greek *pan* meaning 'all'), which translates to *panoramique* in French, making the connection with the panorama explicit (adding *horāma*, sight, from *horān*, to see, hence 'sight of all', implying that everything is available to vision). Even before the word was used, probably around the turn of the 19th century, for the painted panorama, Horace-Bénédict de Saussure, in his *Voyages dans les Alps* (1779-96), referred, in Bernard Comment's words, "to panoramic viewpoints from which the whole of a landscape could be recaptured at a glance," and devised a way in which a 360-degree view could be represented on the page.[10] But the mountains are also a site of resistance. It is this duality that will be explored in *Ariana*, where there is both a struggle for the panorama, and a resistance to the panoramic as such. The film is about the failure to achieve a panoramic representation of the landscape of Afghanistan. This failure is inscribed in a 'panoramic desire' which is more complex than a concentration on its strategic implications would suggest. As well as being an historical form of topographic representation, with a particular genealogy going back to the camera obscura and other aids to landscape rendition and forward to the cinema and on to IMAX, panoramas epitomise a

structure of desire, the desire for totality, for the transformation of the world into a total, unbroken image, with the subject at its centre. This desire is paradoxical, since it is both a desire for the Other, and a desire to reduce the Other to the same.[11]

This duality articulates itself around the idea of the horizon. It has been argued that the origin of the panorama coincides with the discovery of the horizon as a unique experience. In his *Italian Journal* Goethe wrote in the entry of March 30, 1787, on his first sea voyage:

No one who has never seen himself surrounded on all sides by nothing but the sea can have a true conception of the world and his own relation to it. The simple, noble line of the marine horizon has given me, as a landscape painter, quite new ideas.[12]

The horizon is that limit within which the world becomes a representation for the subject. It is a limit that travels with the subject, who is thus placed at the centre of the world understood as picture. As Hegel argued, as soon as a limit is posited, it is gone beyond.[13] The project of the West is to extend the limit by passing beyond it, infinitely. This would be a utopia of totalisation, in which everything would be a potential object for knowledge, everything reduced to a being-for-the-subject, even if that totalisation is necessarily deferred.

Clearly the panorama has historical, ontological and ethical implications, all of which are engaged by Hugonnier's film. If we ask the question 'Why does the panorama need to be interrupted?' the answer might include reference to its historical links with surveillance and military power; or it might refer to the Other, and the religious and ethical prohibition of the image (particularly, in this case, considering Afghanistan's Islamic heritage); or it might refer to the interruption of the homogeneity of the image by an Outside that impels the interstices of the film *Ariana*, the frames of black, to take on an autonomy, rather than being the invisible linkages between two clips of film.

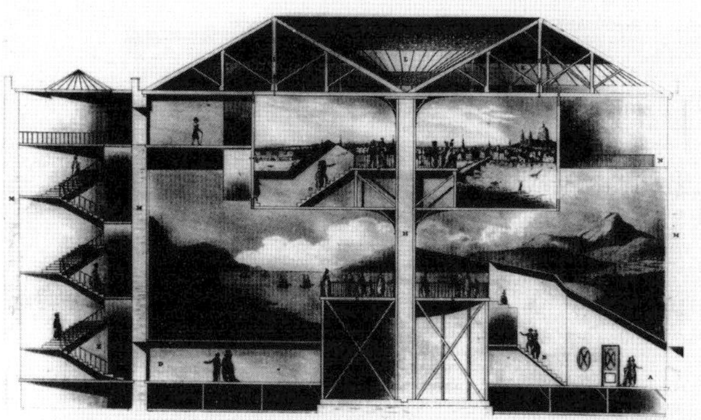

Cross section of Robert Barker's two-level panorama rotunda in Leicester Square,
London, ca. 1798
Stephan Oettermann, *The Panorama: History of a Mass Medium*, New York: Zone Books,
1997, p.104.

The physiological exigencies of the panorama anticipate
aspects of cinema. Painted panoramas were constructed with a
viewing platform and a barrier to keep visitors at a sufficient
distance so that the eye could not discriminate the surface of the
canvas from the image, just as the phenomenon of persistence of
vision is used to suppress the blackness on the celluloid between
the photograms. In both cases the physiology of vision is exploited
in order to maintain the seamless continuity of the representation.
While there is clearly a distinction between the panorama and the
cinematic pan, since the panorama is a laterally unframed image
while film maintains its frame (which is different in its effects
from the frame of both painting and still photography), moving
the image within it, both panorama and pan imply a similar temporal
condition, not least since the 'still' image of the panorama requires
time to consume it by walking around the central platform. Both
imply a continuous, homogenous time (a homogeneity that becomes
the near-instantaneity of global, satellite time). The difference is
that, while the apparatus of the panorama limits it to this positing
of a temporal homogeneity, the pan is only one option for the
shot, and the shot itself is subject to cutting and montage. The
homogenous time of the pan may be disrupted within the cinematic
form itself.

After the first failure to get the panoramic shot, in the Pandjshêr
Valley, "for a couple of days we became nothing more than tourists."
Of course, their panoramic desire, as well as being connected with
the drive to knowledge, had already, as a spectatorial relationship
to the landscape, turned them into tourists. The crew go to Kabul
where, by contrast with the countryside and the mountains which
are shot in 16mm, an 8mm camera is used for the city, intensifying
the sense of fragility and fragmentation. Apart from battles, two
favourite subjects for panoramas were exotic, far-away places –
anticipations of the tourist gaze rooted in imperialism – and, from
the start, the local cityscape. One reason for the mass appeal in the
19th century of panoramas of the surrounding city was that they

allowed the visual mastery of an urban fabric rendered opaque,
fragmented and inescapable by modernisation.[14] In *Ariana* the
first visit to the city is contrasted by a second sequence, which
comes after the claim that utopias are a thing of the past, where
fragmentation is given a positive valency against panoramic
homogeneity. The city is an 'assembly' of the traces of utopian
ideologies, "all of them scattered in fragments." In one of the
city sequences, a series of shots with a hand-held 8mm camera,
where the effect of the moving camera places us within the
fragmentation and flow of what we are seeing, is contrasted
with a pan with the camera fixed on a tripod.

The continuity of this shot, this panorama, seemed to erase
those fragments./It made the cityscape homogenous as
opposed to this urban reality,/as if the idea of discontinuity,
or of a revolution, was impossible.

This contrast is reminiscent of Walter Benjamin's distinction
between the homogenous time of historicism (of which the
panorama is the visual modality), and the 'dialectical image'
in which there is a spark of profane illumination between
discontinuous times. On the subject of panoramas, Benjamin
writes that their 'particular pathos' concerns the relation they
set up between nature and history.[15] If, in the panorama, history
becomes a second nature, then a counter-panoramic mode would
present nature as intervening in history, which is not quite the
same as seeing 'nature' as a historical category. The mountains
with no name seem, for Hugonnier, to offer something other than
a picturesque accompaniment to the naturalisation of history —
"This landscape is never to be seen simply as décor or background."

The panorama creates its reality-effect by combining distance
with detail: the viewer is maintained at a distance from the canvas
in order to preserve the illusion, yet at the same time each detail
is painted with the same attention. Comment writes of a 'double

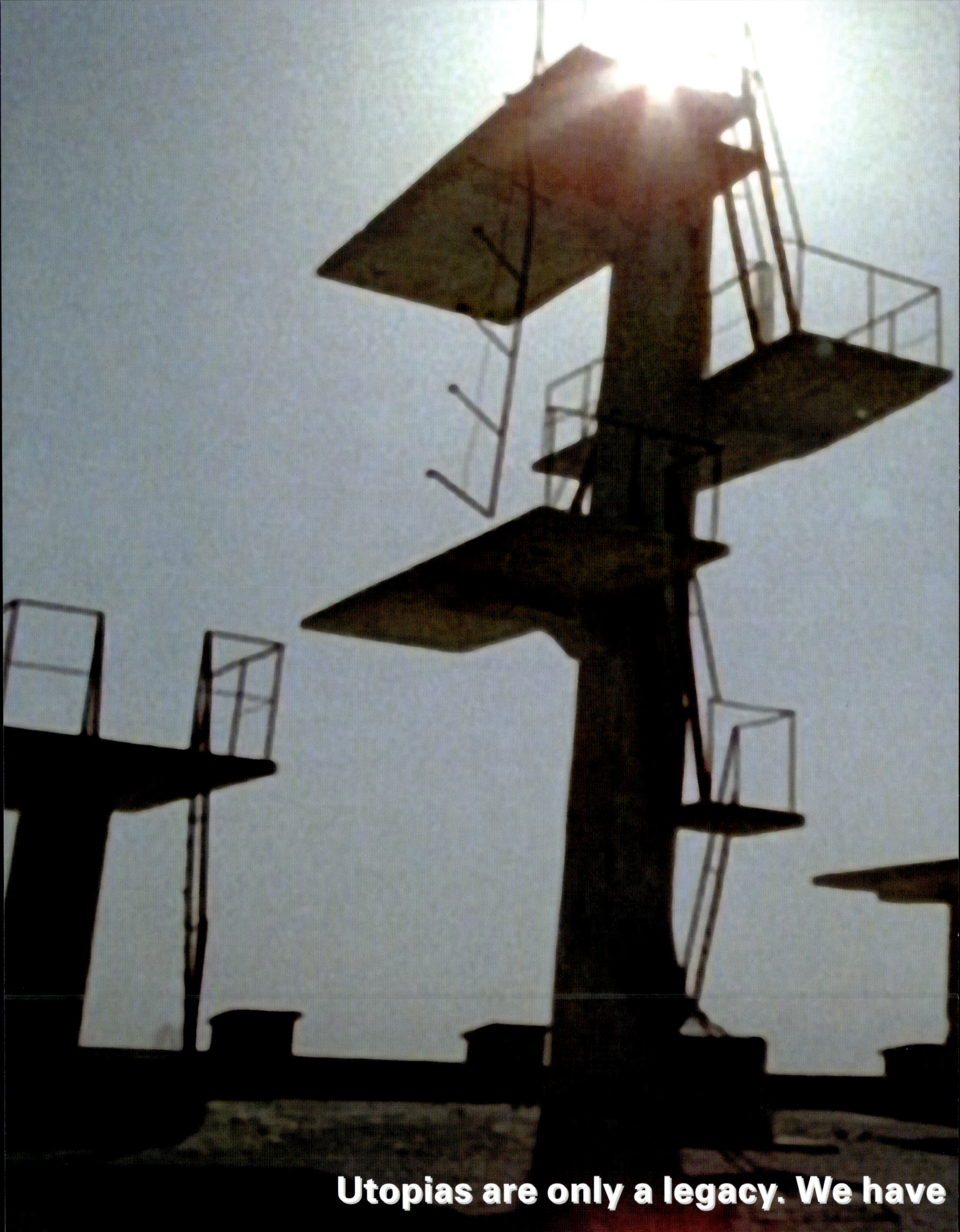
Utopias are only a legacy. We have

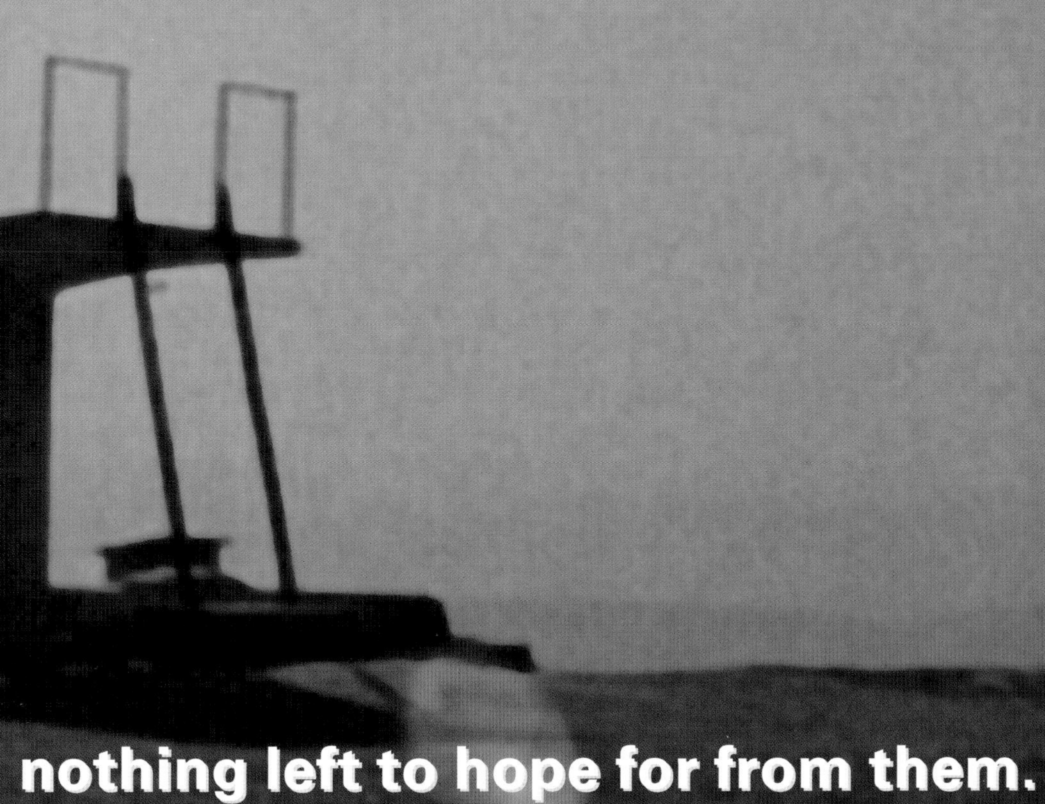

nothing left to hope for from them.

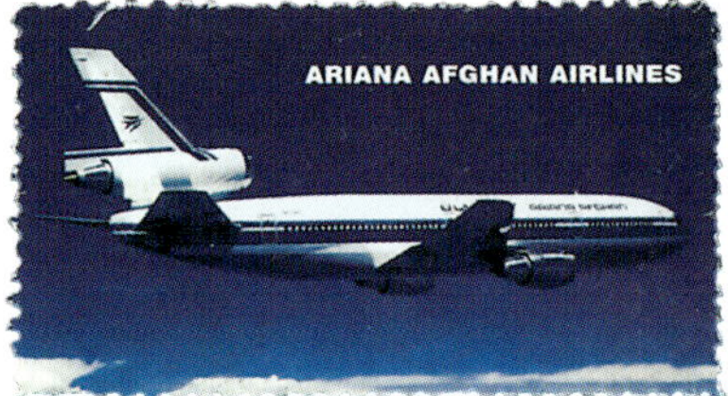

Stamp made for invitation envelopes for the show at
Galerie Yvon Lambert, Paris Oct/Nov 2003

focus' of the panorama: "the panorama was able to combine what could be seen close up with what could be seen in the distance through a conflation of the gaze which rendered the spectator's movement towards the painting unnecessary."[16] Cinema has the possibility of varying the *relation* with distance and nearness through the focal length of the lenses used. A long lens will create the effect of nearness with that which is far away, while a short lens will position the viewer close to the subject. Just this contrast is explored in a montage in *Ariana* which cuts from a group of men sitting drinking tea and talking, shot with a long lens – which implies both surveillance and tourism – to a tracking shot that moves across from a curtained window to a woman's head-scarf and cheek. It is as if we move from being far yet near, to near yet far: while the first sequence offers a false closeness, the second sequence, which puts us beside the woman, nevertheless reminds us of the difference between nearness and proximity — however close we are to the woman, she remains other.

The painted panorama has a potential that is repressed in cinema: the possibility of reversal; since, even if the viewing platform simulates a tower or a mountain-top, the viewers are in the visible – visible to each other, and potentially at least from the field of the panorama itself – in a way that is elided in cinema. The technological passage from panorama to satellite surveillance therefore requires the mediation of cinema, with its unseen viewer (who is regarded not by the reversed look, but by the asymmetric gaze of the Other). In the form of the panorama, however, what the reversibility of the look indicates is the way in which the visitor, who has come in search of a certain mastery of the surroundings, is trapped as the subject of a purely visual simulation (the panorama takes representation into simulation since the illusion is totalised — the frame is removed, in order to avoid comparison of the image with reality). Jeremy Bentham's *panopticon*, a design for a prison, dates from 1791, four years after Barker's patent for the panorama, and is based on a similar idea of total, yet one-sided, visibility, this

time to a warder at the centre of a circle of cells who is invisible to the prisoners, so that they can never be sure whether they are observed, an uncertainty that effects an internalisation of the system of surveillance, in the name of their reform. Olivier Grau remarks that in the panorama "[t]he situation of Bentham's Panopticon is reversed…[t]he observer is the object of political control."[17] Only in this case control is combined with a totalisation of the visual simulation, which would need to be broken by discourse and mutual interaction. Hugonnier's deconstruction of the pan works in two directions: on the side of its connection with the panorama, through the blocking of the view in the name of the other; and on the side of the temporal medium of film, through the interstices (which I will discuss further below). Panoramic desire is simultaneously provoked and thrown into question. This structure of desire is also taken up in relation to the name. It is here that we can begin to discern more clearly the friction, and the play, between the panoramic and the *utopic*.[18]

'Ariana' is the name of the national airline of Afghanistan. It was also the name for the eastern provinces of the ancient Persian Empire, the regions south of the Oxus River — so the modern airline is named after an ancient province that no longer exists, as if the no-longer could connect with the not-yet. The film begins with an airplane sound over black leader, followed by a rather bleak and apparently barren mountain range. The voice-over tells us that "In this country mountains have no name./You cannot tell them apart unless you group them together." Then, over black leader again, the voice says: "During the war, battles were fought to secure vantage points offering panoramas. This was the way to control the country." Then we see a hand covering the lens of the camera, obscuring our view (anticipating all those frustrations in the search for the image), followed by a plane of the Afghan airline on the ground — as if the one from which the film crew had embarked. Then the words: "This was the way to control the country. Planes had to be destroyed." Finally: "ARIANA". The name, as well as being that of the airline, itself homophonous for us with 'air', is the name of a woman; it also resonates with the privative 'a' of the a-topia (non-place) that is one side of u-topia. It is spoken as if it were the addressee of the voice, the beloved, maybe the beloved of a woman, since the voice is a woman's.[19] The voice we hear on the film may or may not be the artist, or the fictional film director who remains unnamed among the crew ("The ones remaining are the anthropologist, the geographer, the cameraman, the sound engineer and the local guide"), or perhaps someone else entirely. The introduction of the possibility of fiction unsettles the objectification implicit in the documentary mode. The danger of documentary is the same as that of historicism (which was the discursive frame for panorama in the 19th century): namely an identification of the signified with the referent in a way that fixes 'reality' as that which is somehow inevitable. The insinuation of fiction separates reality from itself, introducing a distance, drawing attention to the partiality of representation, and opening up a space of possibility for the 'no-place' of utopia.[20]

This question of the relation of referent to signified is developed in the film as a practice of naming. It is as if the name 'Ariana' were the counterpoint to the unnamed mountains. The double invocation of the 'no-name' and the proper name allows us to connect the relation of language to the original gesture towards the singular to the 'uncolonised' space of utopia. If the identification of a place depends on the name, the unnamed mountains maintain themselves, in a sense, as 'no-place'. The word 'utopia' can be derived both from the Greek for 'no place' and for 'good place': it is both a negation and an affirmation at the same time, therefore neutralising the logic of opposition.[21] To introduce a 'no-place' into the mapped, named and described places of the world – and the 'exotic' has served as the provocation for just such an imperialist project, a project that from all sides repeatedly stumbled over Afghanistan – is to open a space for utopia, as 'good place'. Such a space would be of a peculiar kind, since it would have to interrupt the continuity at

which the mapping of 'panoramic' space aims. It would be a space that interrupts space, and since interruption has a temporal dimension, this would amount to an irruption of time into space. If desire needs an object, yet must not 'objectify' that object, turn it into a fetish, in the sense of a false god, then 'Ariana' might name the impossible non-object of utopian desire. It is also, mundanely, the name of the rather run-down Afghan airline, and is therefore inscribed in a specific history of statehood, and the possibility for Afghans to attain their own access to power and a place in the international world. The film works on an edge between the actual politics of the everyday world and a kind of absolute claim, a utopia that cannot be reduced to any of the historical 'utopias' whether Communist, religious or consumerist. Over the image of a ruined, dried-up concrete swimming pool, with the diving boards filmed from below in heroic Constructivist fashion, a passage of voice-over goes:

> All throughout our trip back to the city, our guide told us about his country, his hopes, while promises of past ideologies filled the landscape. / We grew up insulated by liberalism. We have no political ideology anymore. No project. / Utopias are only a legacy. We have nothing left to hope for from them.

The 'we' speaks the despair of a generation in the West that watches the news from Afghanistan, or Iraq, on CNN or BBC, without being able to connect it to a collective political project of resistance. Yet the film also works against this despair in its maintenance of utopic desire, the desire that goes under the name 'Ariana', and is willing to leave the mountains unnamed.

Utopic desire must neutralise the terms of opposition that have determined the historically existing attempts to realise utopia. This interruption is a *formal* operation, a work in and on the medium. Interruption works in a multiplicity of ways in Hugonnier's film. First, there is the simple interruption of the cut within sequences, which tends to evoke a contact, for example between a far and a near view, or between the world of men and that of women. Second, there are the sequences of black leader. Sometimes the soundtrack continues over these, with or without the voice-over in French. Often these black sequences contain the English subtitles. Once we read "(Distant explosions)" but hear no sounds. In this recourse to written description, which is in effect a caption that follows the image, and that is in a certain sense without image, writing takes on an autonomy, as if the black screen were a negation of the image, that requires an alternative expression, one that would not fetishise what is represented. A further complication is introduced if we know, or perhaps sense, that the following sequence, which included flashes of red, was not in fact footage of a battle: this insinuates into the film a certain undecidability between fact and fiction.

If the pan is understood as a modality of documentary, then the question arises both of the status of what we are seeing, and of the objectifying implications of documentary, its reduction of otherness to image, which has been contested in the films of Jean Rouch, including fabulations created by the subject-participants themselves as well as foregrounding the position and involvement of the anthropologist: truth is not objectively given in facts and data, but provoked through fiction and enactment. Jean-Luc Godard mentioned Rouch's 1957 film *Moi, un noir* in support of his dictum that "all great fiction films tend towards documentary, just as all great documentaries tend towards fiction."[22] Godard also contrasted Rouch to the 'classicist' film-makers Eisenstein and Hitchcock: "The others, people like Rouch, don't know exactly what they are doing, and search for it. The film is the search."[23] It is no coincidence, then, that the team in *Ariana* that sets out to film in Afghanistan includes not only a geographer (recalling the topographic origins of panorama), but also an anthropologist. In traditional terms – critiqued by Rouch and others – these are emblematic of those who set out to transform the land and those who inhabit it into objects of discursive knowledge, a project that, in the course of

Hugonnier's film, remains frustrated with the inaccessibility of the panorama. The possibility of another kind of relation is suggested by the film show to which the crew is invited: what is presented is a film of tropical fish swimming in their habitat (Afghanistan does not have a coastline, so this is another desired, inaccessible point of view). The camera moves underwater, 'with' the fish, yet at the same time the viewer is separated. The image is ambivalent: on the one hand, the 'medium' provides the possibility of a connection with the Other and the alien[24]; on the other hand, the immersive is the form that is anticipated by the panorama, culminating in the rotunda Claude Monet specified for his *Waterlilies* — he wanted to decorate a drawing-room in a way that 'would have produced the illusion of a whole without end, of a wave without horizon and without shore... a haven for quiet meditation at the centre of a flower-filled aquarium."[25] So this sequence could provide an alternative to the panorama, or its destiny: being-with-the-other, or immersive experience with no outside, undecidably. What the underwater sequence in the film-show presents is immersion without totality; tellingly it is followed by the city shots using a hand-held camera.

Finally, permission is obtained to climb 'Television Hill' — we are shown the letter of permission being written in Arabic script, reminding us of the role of calligraphy in a culture that restricts the image, in contrast to the global dissemination of the image through broadcasting (near the beginning of the film we hear, on the soundtrack, a snatch of the London news). In this last attempt in the story to attain a panoramic representation we are shown a view from above the city to the mountains – although not a pan – and told that "The entire landscape was like a still image, a painting. / This spectacle made us euphoric and gave us a feeling of totality." In the painted panoramas, it was both important both that the view from the platform be uninterrupted, and that the visitors, as the subjects of a homogenous view, form a unity, a collective subject. The ideology of the panorama was in effect to unify the publics of the 19th century nation-states of the West in the age of imperialism. Here, however, the summit is shared with the Afghan soldier who has accompanied the crew and "stood proudly in front of the view." It is as if his presence in the image reflects attention back onto the 'invisible' film crew, and interposes a difference where there may have been a presupposition of unity. This provokes the question of who 'owns' the view: if the viewers are not one, who has the right (remembering the earlier legal transaction of the 'permission') to this point of view, this panorama? The film crew must abjure the temptation of euphoria, the lure of totality. Whereupon, "We gave up filming." The screen goes black.

Is this a moment of frustration, or an act of self-denial? At stake is whether we can still – or once again – speak of an ethics and politics of form. In a group discussion about Marguerite Duras' and Alain Resnais' film *Hiroshima mon amour* (1959) in the year that it appeared, Jean-Luc Godard stated that "tracking shots are a question of morality."[26] The question of the ethical and political implications of a particular kind of shot was taken up two years later by Jacques Rivette, in a review of Guillo Pontecorvo's film *Kapo* entitled 'De l'abjection',[27] where the question was that of a forward tracking shot when a character commits suicide: "Look at *Kapo*, the shot when Emmanuelle Riva commits suicide by throwing herself on the electrified wires: someone who decides at that moment to do a forward tracking shot to reframe the body from beneath, taking care to set the raised hand exactly in a corner of the final frame, deserves nothing more than the deepest contempt."[28] The critic Serge Daney returned to the controversy around this claim in his essay 'Le traveling de Kapo',[29] where he adds, "Thus a simple camera movement was the one not to make. The movement you must – *obviously* – be abject to make. As soon as I read those lines I know the author was absolutely right."[30] That *Kapo* is, as Daney states at the outset "among the movies I have never seen," far from qualifying his statement, reinforces it, since there are things that should not be shown, or at least are not to be represented in an image that does not speak of its own limitations. But is Rivette still right today? The moment of assent to this doctrine is situated by Daney in relation to his own birth as a cinephile at a time when, between Auschwitz and Hiroshima in the near past, and the looming threat of nuclear annihilation, the essential thing seemed to be an aesthetics and politics of form. Daney contrasts the tracking shot in *Kapo*, a camera-movement that aestheticizes a dead body in a way that obliterates singularity, with the distance maintained by Resnais' film on the Holocaust, *Nuit et Brouillard* (1955), although he sees the way in which that film is wheeled out as a touchstone whenever anti-semitism is raised in France as problematic, and the piles of bodies in that film too close to the pornographic beauty of the Western Christian tradition of painting. A less reserved contrast is with Mizoguchi's *Ugetsu* (1959), where Miyagi's death "seems so accidental that the camera almost misses it." The final movement of Daney's essay begins with the image of the video of the 1985 Live Aid concert: "The rich singers (*"We are the world, we are the children!"*) were mixing their image with the image of the skinny children. Actually they were taking their place; they were replacing and erasing them."[31] Does the lesson of the immorality of the tracking shot in *Kapo* still apply? "In *Kapo* it was still possible to be upset at Pontecorvo for inconsiderately abolishing a distance he should have 'kept'. The tracking shot was immoral for the simple reason that it was putting us – him filmmaker and me spectator – in a place where we did not belong, where I anyway could not and did not want to be, because he 'deported' me from my real situation as a spectator-witness forcing me to be part of the picture. What was the meaning of Godard's formula if not that *one should never put himself where one isn't nor should he speak for others?*" We should be careful not to equate this distance with detachment. Cinema 'adopted' him, Daney writes, "So that it could teach me to tirelessly touch with my gaze the distance from me at which the other begins."[32] In this distance resides the distinction between identification, with the consolations of sympathy, and respect for the other as other.

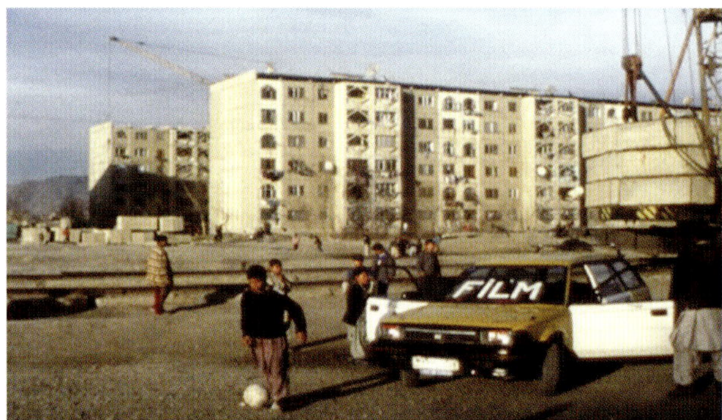
End credits image, *Ariana*

In *Ariana*, Marine Hugonnier shows herself to be concerned in an exemplary way with the "distance from me at which the other begins." Is not the problem with the pan, finally acknowledged on 'Television Hill', precisely that it would put us "in a place where we did not belong"? Just over a decade after the moment when for Daney, who died of AIDS in 1992, the year the aforementioned essay was published, it seemed that "tracking shots are no longer a moral issue" and "cinema is too weak to entertain such a question," Hugonnier returns, in the context of a new imperialism, to the ethics and politics of form.

The final interruption of the panorama gathers together the interruptions at the level of the story, and another level of interruption, which is connected in formal terms with the interruption by the interstice.[33] The 'between' becomes an interstice when its role exceeds that of joining two clips of film, rendering itself invisible or suppressed by means of continuity and suture, for example by maintaining subjective continuity by means of a structure of shot and counter-shot. The interstice ceases to relate to the 'whole' of the film – that implied, if ever-receding, totality of the shots – and refers to the Outside, as its very intervention. It is no coincidence that the intervention of the Outside in the interstices relates to the sense of failure, frustration and lassitude of the film-crew: it is in the context of the failure of their attempt to attain the totalised horizon of the panorama that the 'between' of the images figures as something other than the linkages of continuity and interrupts the seamlessness of representation. The homogenous time of the panorama is related to a past that is 'my' past, and a future that is essentially a projection of the present. As the voice-over says, against an image of the blue sky:

> After all, doesn't a high point of view allow the possibility
> of projecting a future into space?/Wasn't it also the sweet
> memory of the tourist attraction that wasn't to be missed
> on holidays when we were children?

Nostalgia here is related to the transformation of the landscape into an image to be consumed, a 'tourist attraction'. Landscape is transformed into a souvenir out of a denial of loss, which is also the denial of the possibility of a fracture in the continuity of time, of a revolution. The homogeneity of the panorama implies the attempt to control the future by reference to that which was. The interruption of the panorama at the level of the interstice, as an intervention from the Outside, might imply the opening up of the future to the other and the unprecedented, the 'utopic' as distinct from the failed historical utopias, which are 'panoramic' in their attempts at the totalisation of past and future. We are left with the image of the crew's car, 'FILM' taped in large letters on its windscreen, abandoned with its doors open in the midst of an urban housing development. Around it people walk by and local boys play soccer. The shot is a fixed one, which emphasises the non-visibility of the out-of-frame from which passers-by emerge and into which they disappear, and therefore, as opposed to the attempt of the pan to show all, the limits of the image. The credits roll. Life goes on.

Michael Newman teaches in the department of Art History, Theory and Criticism at the School of the Art Institute of Chicago, and writes on contemporary arts and philosophy.

1 David Levi Strauss, *Between the Eyes: Essays on Photography and Politics* (New York: Aperture, 2003), p.190.

2 Olivier Grau, *Virtual Art: From Illusion to Immersion*, (Cambridge, Mass. and (London: The MIT Press, 2003), p.53.

3 Ibid, p.55.

4 Ibid, p.57.

5 See Joëlle Bolloch, *Photographies de guerre* (exhibition catalogue, Paris: Musée d'Orsay, 2004), pp.11-12, and plates 14-19.

6 Hélène Puiseux, *Les figures de la guerre: Représentations et sensibilités 1839-1996* (Paris: Gallimard, 1997), p.94. She concludes concerning the photographs of the Crimean War that "they don't speak of heroism, they don't say that one dies there, they say that one lives there, that one loses time there, that one kills time there and not only human beings" (p.97).

7 See *Voir/ne pas voir la guerre: Histoire des representations photographiques de la guerre* (exhibition catalogue, Paris: Somogy, éditions d'art and Bibliothèque de Documentation Internationale Contemporaine, 2001), pp.38-9.

8 Bolloch, *Photographies de guerre*, p.13.

9 Quotations without a source being given are from the voice-over to *Ariana*.

10 Bernard Comment, *The Panorama* (London: Reaktion Books, 1999), pp.81-2.

11 The great exploration of panoramic desire and its frustration in literature is of course Marcel Proust's *À la recherche du temps perdu*, as is noted in Ibid, p.143.

12 Cited in Stephan Oettermann, *The Panorama: History of a Mass Medium* (New York: Zone Books, 1997), p. 7-8.

13 G.W.F. Hegel, *Hegel's Logic*, trans. William Wallace (Oxford: Clarendon Press, 1975), §60: "No one knows, or even feels, that anything is a limit or defect, until he is at the same time above and beyond it."

14 For a discussion of this, see Comment, *The Panorama*, pp. 134-38.

15 Walter Benjamin, *The Arcades Project* (Cambridge, Mass. and London: Harvard University Press, 1999), p 363. For a discussion of 'dialectical images', see Michael W. Jennings, *Dialectical Images: Walter Benjamin's Theory of Literary Criticism*. (Ithaca and London: Cornell University Press, 1987), p.363.

16 Comment, *The Panorama*, pp.113.

17 Grau, *Virtual Art*, p.111.

18 The term 'utopic' comes from Louis Marin, Louis, *Utopics: The Semiological Play of Textual Spaces* (Atlantic Highlands, N.J.: Humanities Press International, 1984) to which the discussion below is indebted.

19 In this mode of address there is perhaps also a very muted hint at the 13th century love poems of Jalal al-Din Rumi, founder of the Mevlani Sufi order of Whirling Dervishes, who was born in Balkh in what is now Afghanistan, and who offered a way to God through longing and ecstatic sexual passion. The appeal of Rumi, who enjoyed something of a cult in the West during the 1990s, has something to do with a utopian fusion of the spiritual and the sexual. His poems are today frequently to be heard on radio stations in Kabul and Mazar-I-Sharif (See Amy Standen, "Rumi: No.1 in Afghanistan and the USA," in salon.com at http://dir.salon.com/people/feature/2001/10/12/barks/index.html?pn=1

20 See Ibid, pp.86-7.

21 For the relation between utopia and the neutral, see Ibid, pp. 3-30.

22 Cited in Peter Wollen, *Paris Hollywood: Writings on Film* (London: Verso, 2002), p.99.

23 "B.B. of the Rhine" in Jean Narboni and Tom Milne, eds., *Godard on Godard: Critical Writings by Jean-Luc Godard* (New York: Da Capo Press, 1986), p.101, cited in the excellent obituary by Emilie Bickerton, 'The Camera Possessed: Jean Rouch, Ethnographic Cinéaste: 1917-2004', *New Left Review*, second series, no. 27, May-June 2004, pp.49-63.

24 In an email to the author, Hugonnier related this sequence to the nature documentaries of Jean Painlevé, whose film *The Sea Horse* (1934) was one of the first films to use underwater footage.

25 Quoted in Comment, *The Panorama*, p.145.

26 Jean Domarchi, Jacques Doniol-Valcroze, Jean-Luc Godard, Pierre Kast, Jacques Rivette, Eric Rohmer, 'Hiroshima, notre amour', *Cahiers du Cinéma*, no. 97, July 1959 (translated in Jim Hillier ed., *Cahiers du Cinéma: The 1950s: Neo-Realism, Hollywood, New Wave* (Cambridge, Mass.: Harvard University Press, 1985), p.62. Luc Moullet, in an article on Samuel Fuller, had already claimed that "morality is a question of tracking shots" (Luc Moullet, 'Sam Fuller – sur les brisées de Marlowe', *Cahiers du Cinéma*, no.93, March 1959, translated as 'Sam Fuller: In Marlowe's Footsteps' in Hillier, ed., *Cahiers*, p.148).

27 *Cahiers du Cinéma*, 20, June 1961, reprinted in Alain Bergala et al., *Théories du cinema* (Paris: Cahiers du cinema, 2001), pp.37-40.

28 Ibid, p.38.

29 *Traffic*, no. 4, autumn 1992, reprinted in Serge Daney and Serge Toubiana, *Persévérance* (Paris: P.o.l., 1994), pp., 15-39, citations from the English translation by Laurent Kretschmar, 'The Tracking Shot in *Kapo*' at www.sensesofcinema.com/contents/04/30/kapo_daney.html. I thank Pierre Huyghe for drawing my attention to the relevance of this text to the discussion of Hugonnier's film.

30 Daney, *Persévérance*, p.16.

31 Ibid, p.37.

32 Ibid, p.38: "Pour qu'il m'apprenne à toucher inlassablement du regard à quelle distance de moi commence l'autre."

33 My discussion of the interstice is based on Gilles Deleuze, *Cinema 2: The Time-Image* (London: The Athlone Press, 1989), pp. 179-88. For Deleuze, the Outside is time.

Mountains With No Name (Pandjshêr Valley, Afghanistan)

2003
9 lambda prints mounted onto aluminium
126,4 x 133,3 cm

This series of nine photographs is a companion piece to 'Ariana'.
It is a group of portraits of the mountains that surround the
Pandjshêr Valley in the North East of the country. These mountains
have never been named: they remain blank areas on the map where
only the paths are given names by local inhabitants. Their anonymity
runs counter to the Western tradition by which every mountain
is named, a practice that coincided with European imperialism and
the expansion of the colonies. The mountains surrounding the
Pandjshêr Valley exist outside this history.

Shoot   Pandjshêr Valley and Kabul, Afghanistan, August 2002
Camera   6 x 7 Mamiya RZ
Stock   160 Nc portra Kodak
Lens   110 mm Mamiya
Processed   Metro, London
Print   Glorious Productions, London
Aluminium mount and frame   Bliss, London/Darbyshire, London
Production   MW Projects, London

Reproduction   300 dpi scan from original negatives printed offset
litho on Hello matt 170gsm

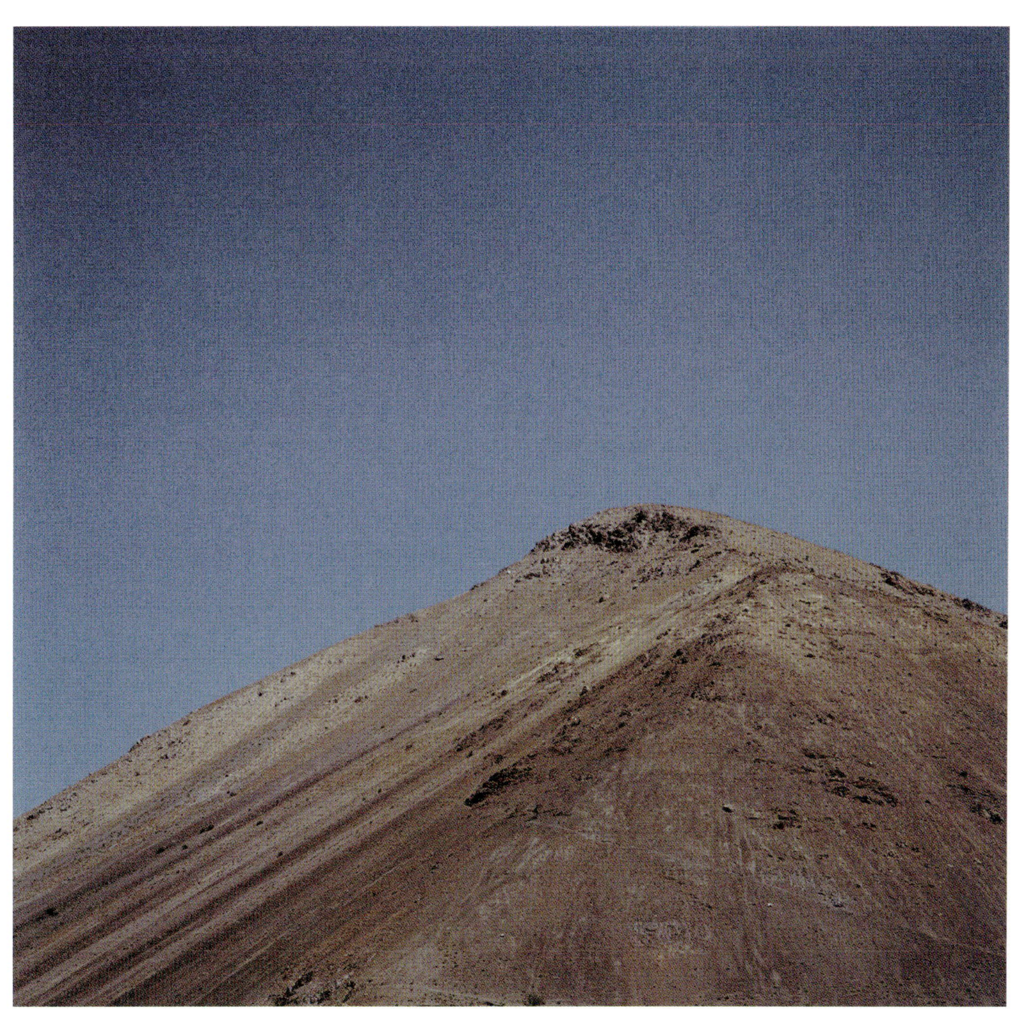

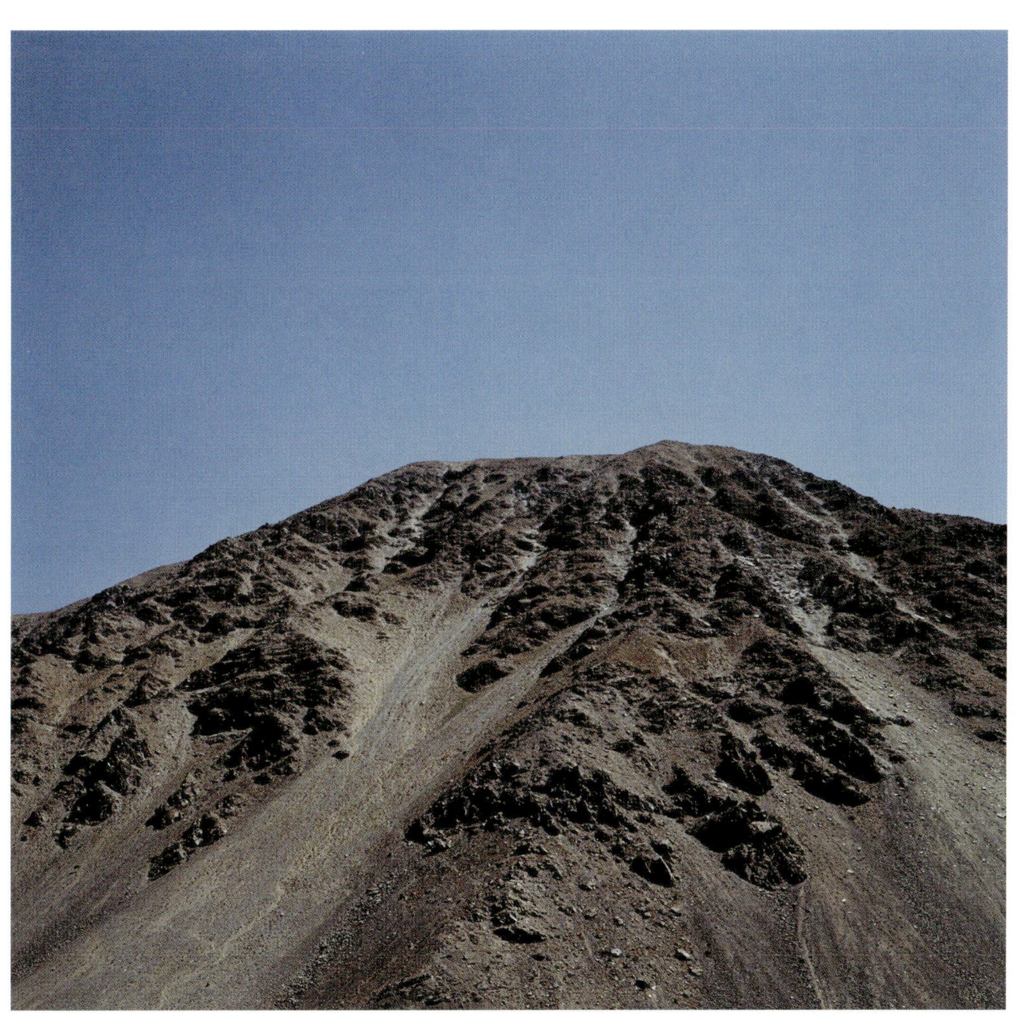

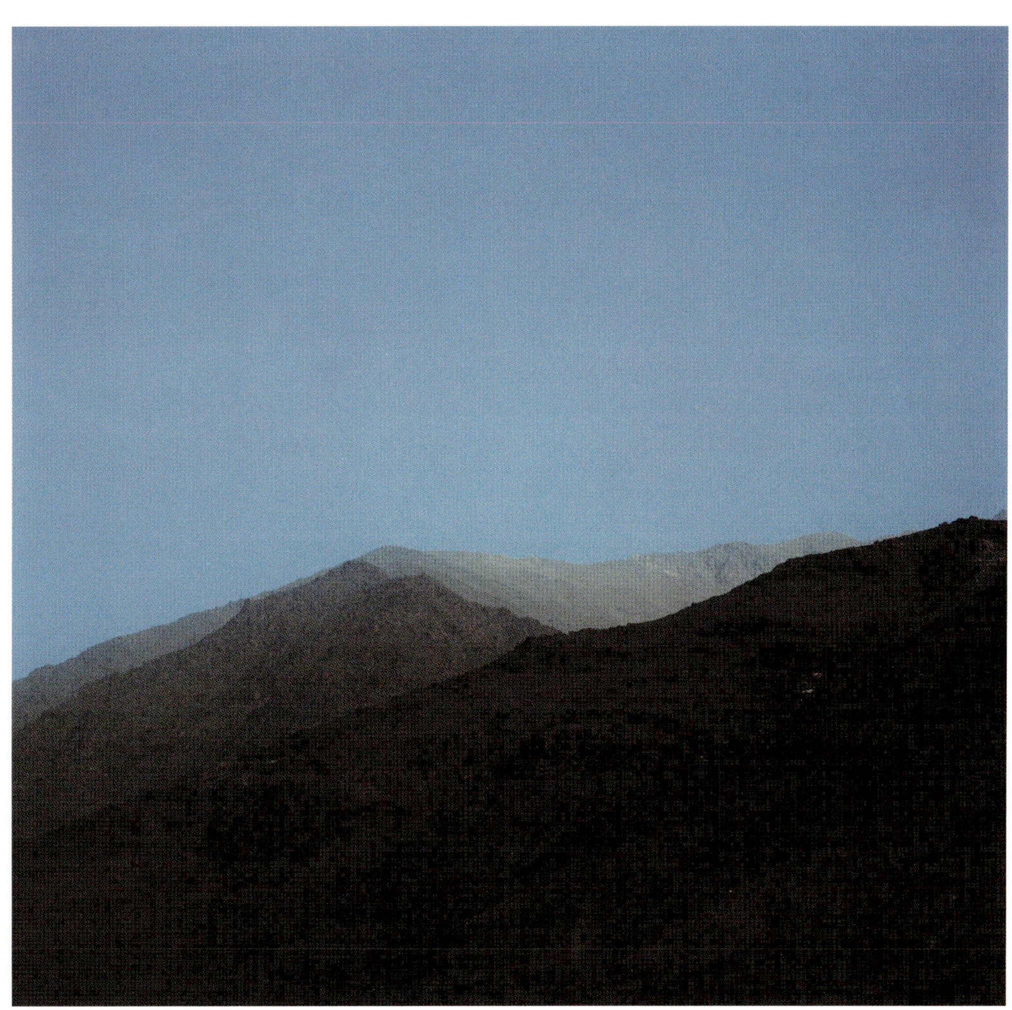

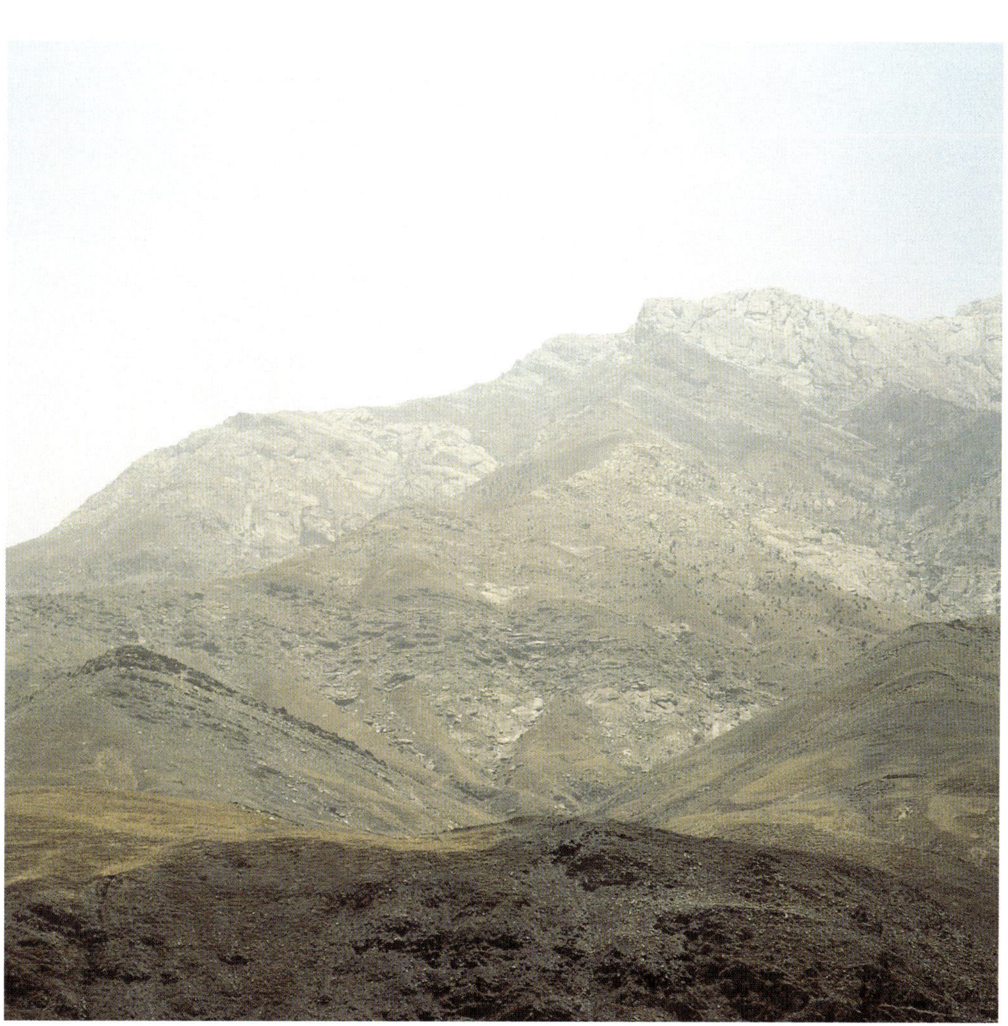

The Last Tour

2004
Super 16mm film transferred onto DVD with sound
Duration 14.17 minutes

'The Last Tour' takes as a point of departure the laws that
increasingly regulate our access to, and perception of, Nature
in our visits to National Parks. The action of this fiction is set
at the end of the Age of Spectacle, at a time when these tourist
attractions are about to be completely closed off to the public.
The viewer embarks on a 'last tour', a hot-air balloon flight over
the famous, iconic Matterhorn in the Swiss Alps. The film suggests
the possibility of a blank space re-appearing on the map, a reference
to the world before the Era of Discovery.

Shoot Zermatt and its surroundings, Switzerland, February 2004 /
Disneyland, Los Angeles, November 2003
Camera Aaton A-minima
Stock 7218/500 asa, 7274/200 asa kodak
Lenses 9.5mm, 12mm, 16mm, 25mm & 50mm Zeiss Primes, 10-100mm
Canon Zoom, 5.7mm Kinoptic.
Aspect ratio 1:85
Director of Photography Tom Townend
Editor Ida Bregninge
Sound Cristian Manzutto
Music Sebastien Roux
Executive Producers Renaud Sabari/APC, Paris
Processed Cinedia, Paris
Post Production Transatlantic Video, Paris
Graded Transat, Paris
Produced by Galerie Judin, Zürich, Dundee Contemporary Arts,
Villa Medicis hors les Murs, Paris

Reproduction 300 dpi scan from original telecinema printed offset
litho on Hello matt 170gsm

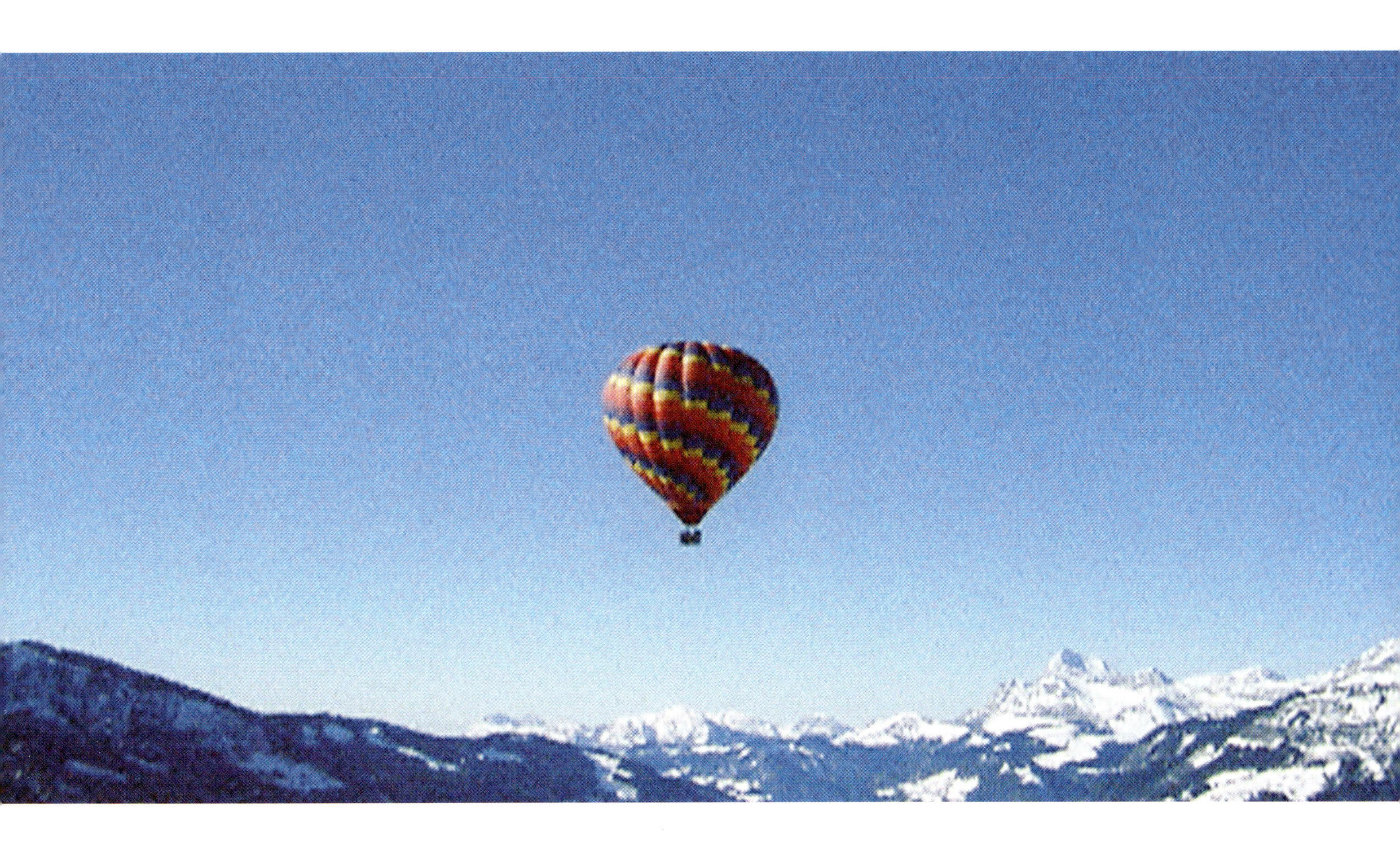

You have a ticket for the Last Tour around
the Matterhorn and its national park.

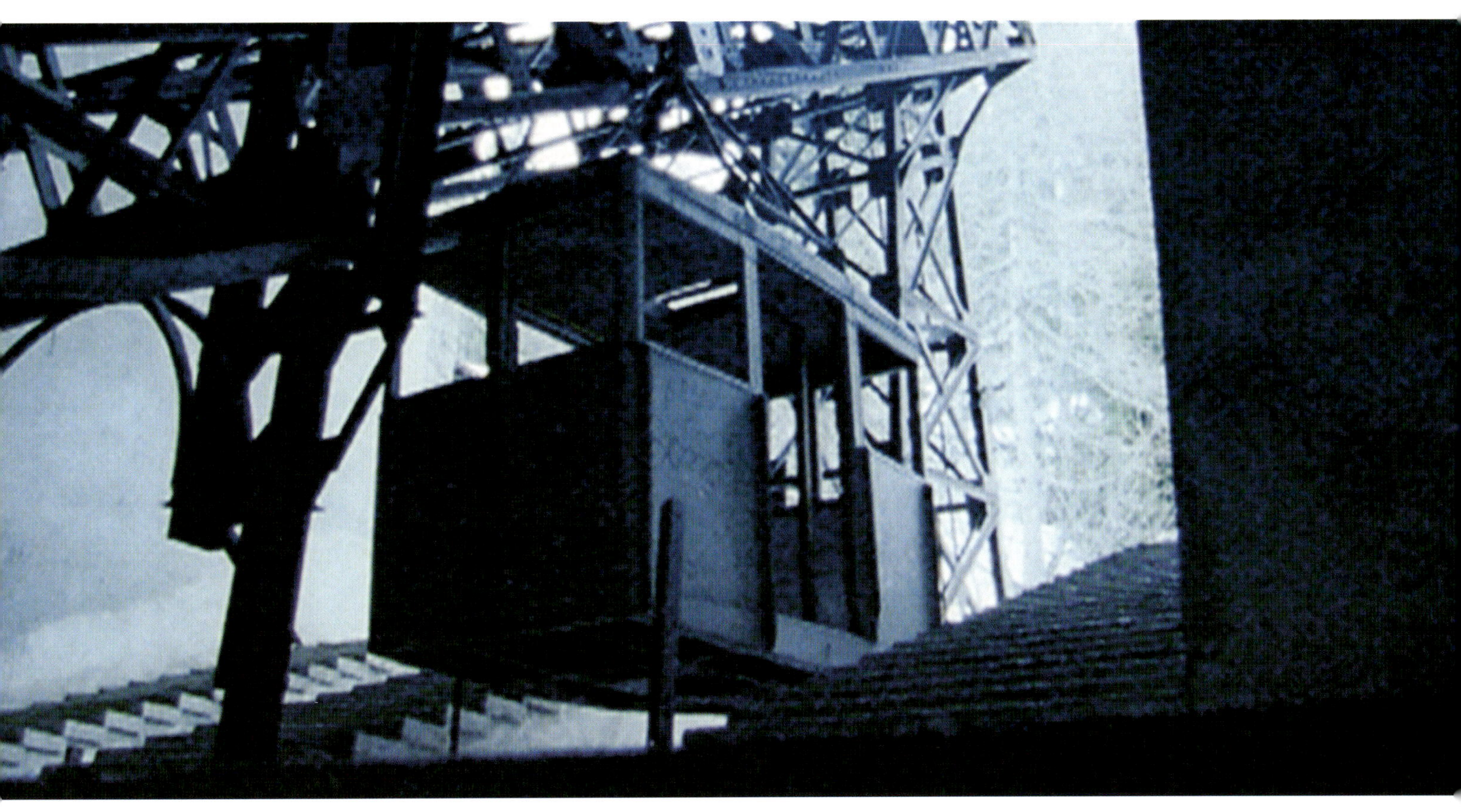

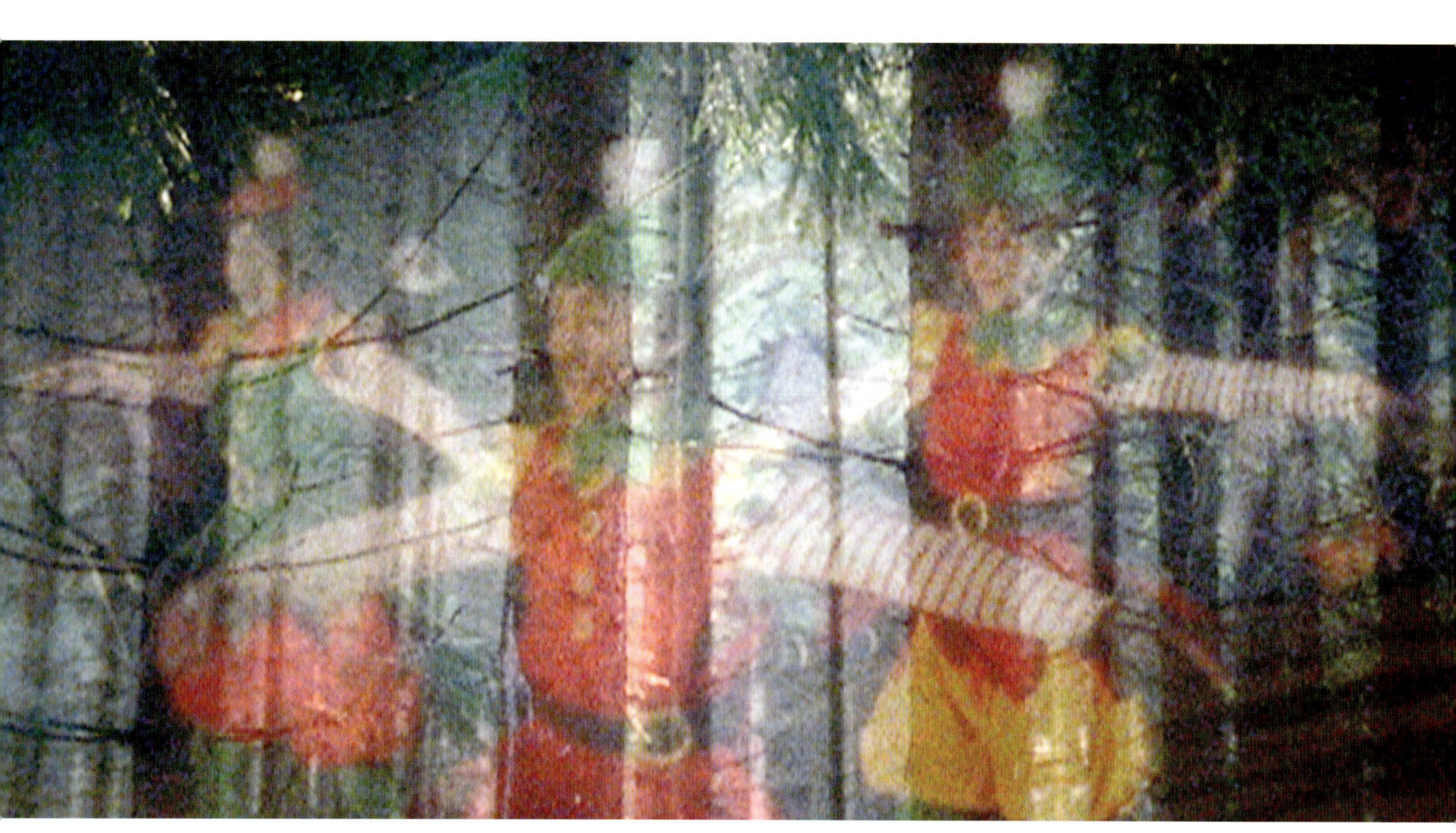

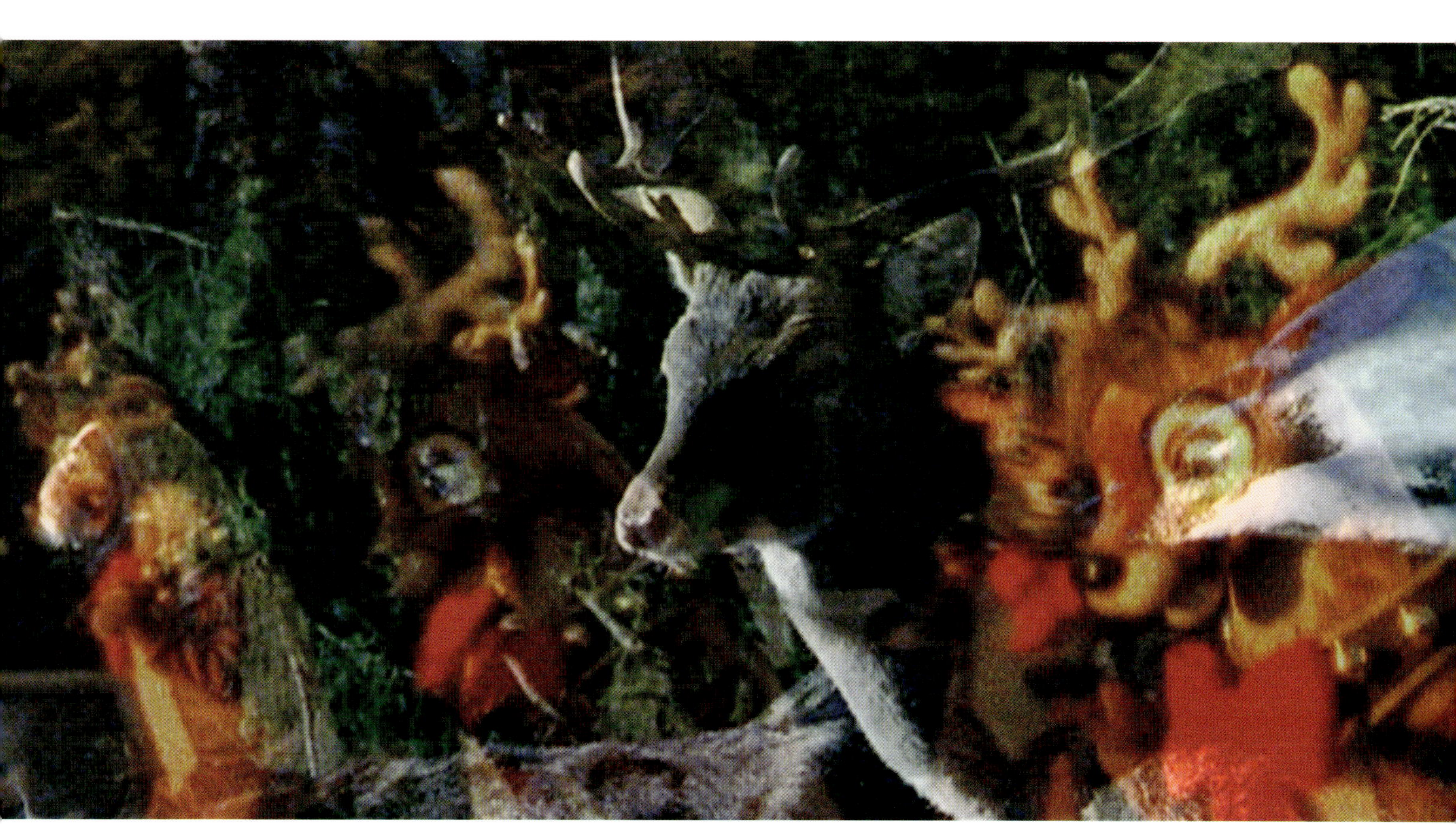

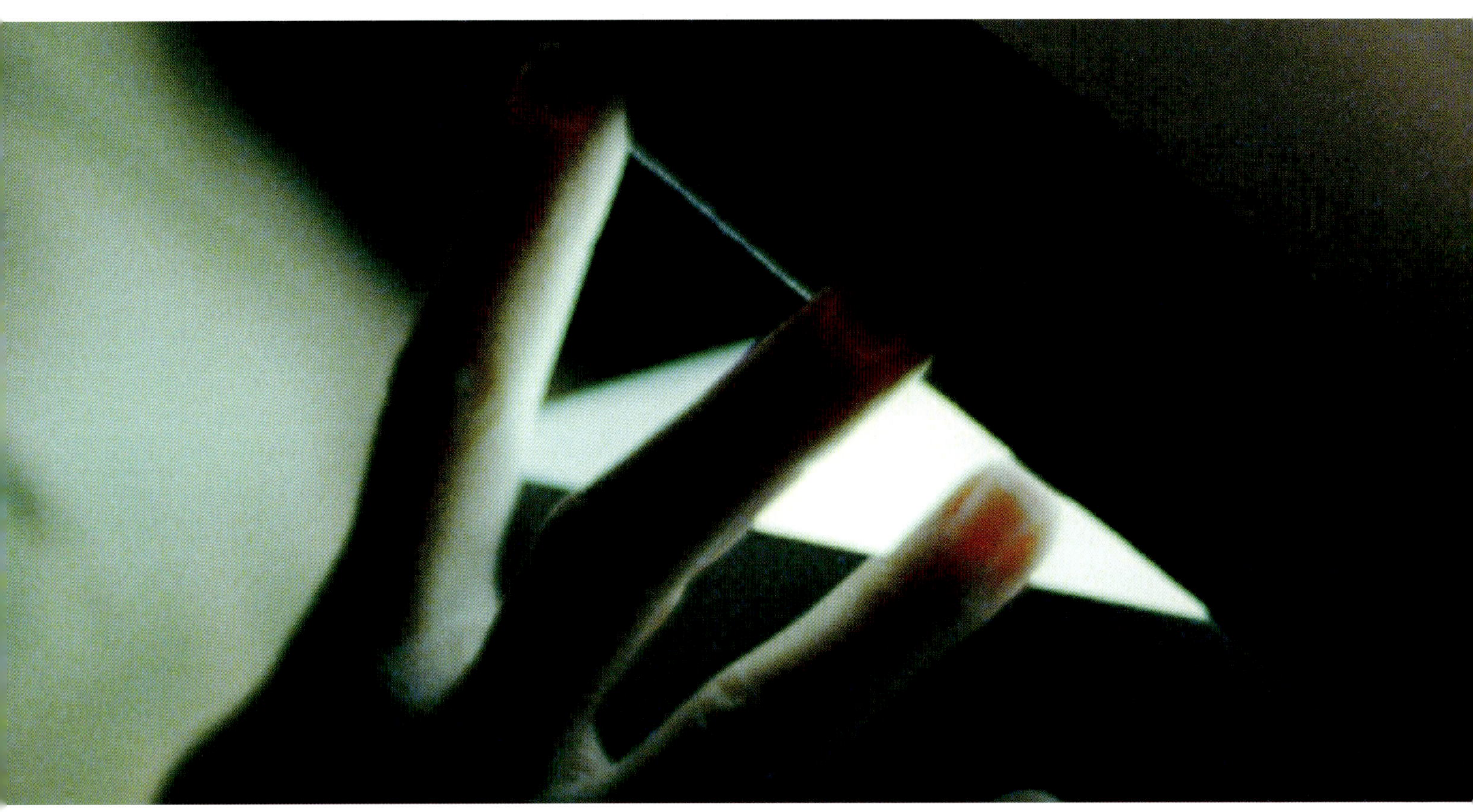

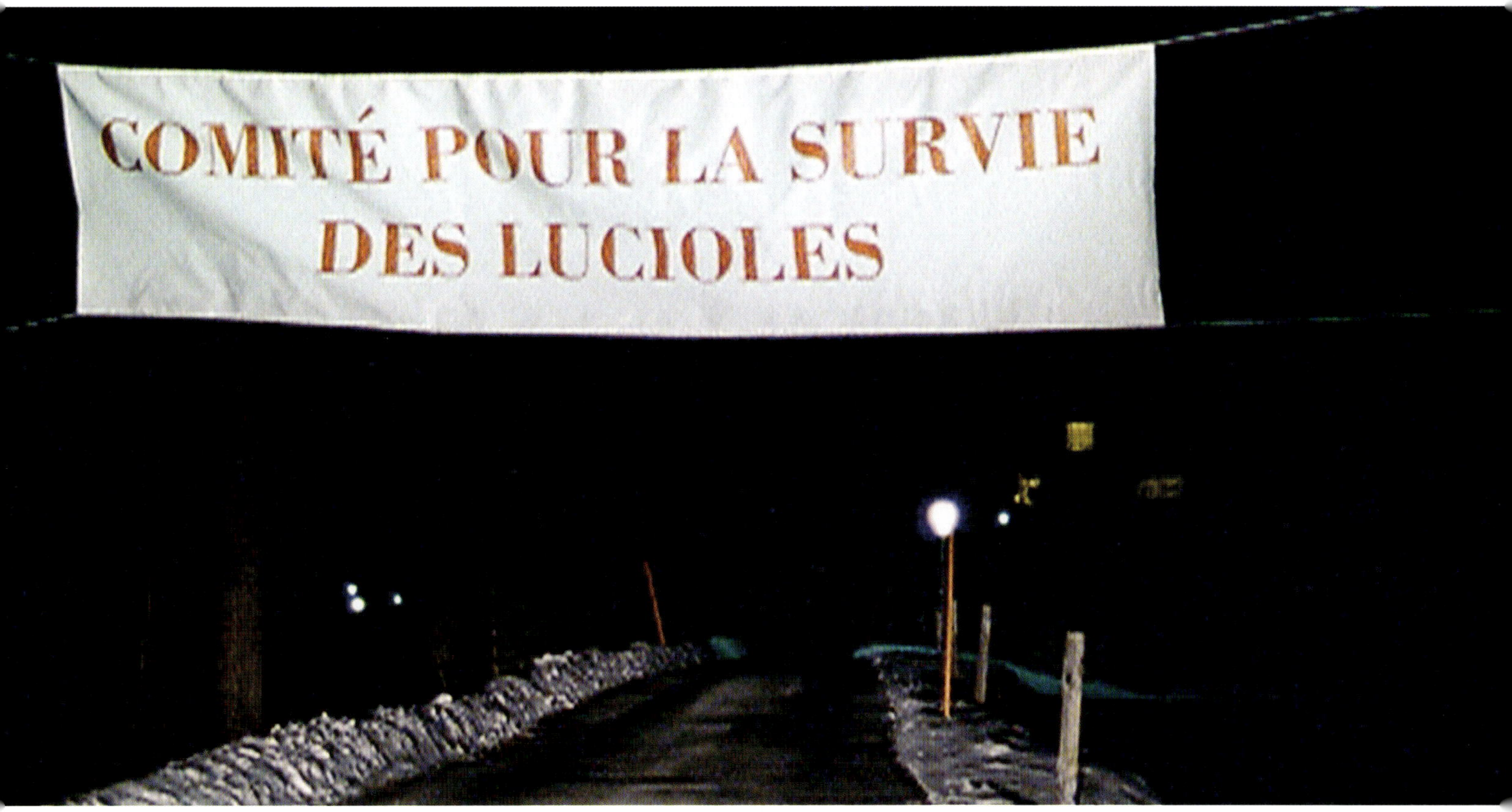

COMITÉ POUR LA SURVIE
DES LUCIOLES

The Beginning and the End Jeremy Millar

'**Mountains are the beginning and the end of all natural scenery**.'
— John Ruskin, *Modern Painters*

'**When we try to pick out anything by itself, we find it hitched to everything else in the universe**.'
— John Muir, *My First Summer in the Sierra* (1911)

'**These Tourists, heaven preserve us!**'
—William Wordsworth, from 'The Brothers' (1800)

At the beginning of Gus Van Sant's film *Gerry* (2002) we follow an old Mercedes along a road that rolls around strangely geometric hills and darts straight across plains. We look back into the car, at the two eponymous characters (played by Casey Affleck and Matt Damon), and then forward to the road once more, before looking back at the two young men as they turn off the road down what seems, judging by the movement of the car, to be an unpaved track. They leave the car and begin to walk across an expanse of scrubland, past bushes and a sign that reads 'Wilderness Trail'. "Hey, Gerry, the path," one calls to the other, although no path seems visible. Shortly afterwards, just as one of them finishes attending to their own call of nature, a small group of women pass them on the track alongside which they are now standing.

"Hiking moms on the trail?"

"It's just gonna be all tourists up there."

"Well how far's the thing?"

"I don't know, we're like halfway there. Let's go this way, man. It's got to… Everything's gonna go to the thing, everything's gonna lead to the same place."

"Just loop around, do our own fresh route."

It need not concern us here as to what happens to them as they leave the trail; however these opening few scenes establish some interesting ideas with regard to our relationship to nature, especially 'wild' nature, and how such a relationship is mediated through leisure and tourism. Such is the subject, also, of Marine Hugonnier's most recent film, *The Last Tour* (2004). Unlike Van Sant's slow accumulation of details, Hugonnier's exposition is boldly stated at the start of the film in simple white text upon a black background, like subtitles, although there is no voice audible of which they are the clarification, only the pained mechanical sound of traffic: "This is about a time where natural sites are so regulated by protective laws/with limited visitor access and restricted view points, that they are becoming almost invisible/The action of the film is set in the near future/where these tourist sites are about to come to a complete closure." For all its clarity, however, it is not without a certain ambiguity. In accepting this situation as its point of departure, the film makes no attempt to explain how it may have arisen, or, indeed, allows for any possibility of such an explanation. Perhaps we might consider it, then, as sharing certain characteristics with other forms of speculative or fantastic fiction. In denying an explanation at this stage, a denial that is maintained throughout, the film begins with an authority that becomes increasingly eroded throughout its duration, or, as the critic Mikhail Bakhtin put it in his study on Dostoevsky, "The fantastic serves here not in the positive *embodiment* of the truth, but in the search after the truth, its provocation and, most importantly, its *testing*."

The camera is low on the front of a moving car, its headlights illuminating the road as it heads through a tunnel. The tarmac has been repaired in places, and the sodium lights sometimes reflected in the wet of the tarmac like a series of chemical sunsets. There are three shots of quiet woodland, amongst trees — perhaps this is what might be found high above the speeding vehicles below? The screen returns to black – "You are sitting in the back of a car"– and though the noise of the road rises once more, and we seem to have left tranquil nature behind, it is that to which we are in fact travelling. "You have a ticket for the Last Tour around the Matterhorn and its national park," we read against the black, and then we see the mountain, its acute peak appearing almost as a geological archetype,

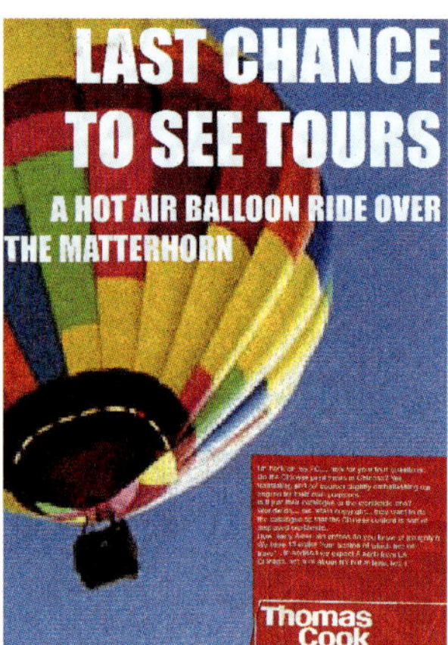

Prop for the shoot of *The Last Tour*

or something of our own imagining. Perhaps it is. The screen is black and the road noise returns: "Your mind is drifting."

It seems unsurprising that such an image would appear in the mind's eye as somehow emblematic of natural beauty, and yet our attraction to wild landscape in general, and mountains in particular, is actually quite a recent development in western culture, and a development which it is important to explore briefly in the context of Hugonnier's film. The letter written in 1336 by Petrarch, the Italian poet, to his father, in which he describes his climbing of Mt. Ventoux in France, is considered the first documented ascent for pleasure, yet the mountains were considered ugly, dangerous, even immoral places for centuries to come. These were places inhabited by monsters, or by groups of people seen as equally hostile, such as the tribe of Assassins in Sir John Mandeville's famous *Travels* (1366), the Zapoletes, a "hideous, savage and fierce race" who dwell "in the high mountains" of Thomas More's *Utopia* (1516), or the *banditti* found within the brooding paintings of the Salvator Rosa (1615–73), and with whom he was said to associate. We might even consider our rather more recent imagery of those moving amongst the mountains, such as Osama Bin Laden, or the Chechen terrorist Shamil Basayev. Indeed, there appeared something diabolical about being on a mountain summit, and the views which such a position afforded, particularly when we consider that the most extensive panoramas of the 17th century are to be found in John Milton's *Paradise Regained* (1665–7), with Satan showing Christ all the kingdoms of the earth from a mountaintop. (Perhaps we might keep this episode in mind while considering Hugonnier's recent film *Ariana*, which also explores the relationship between power and the panoramic overview, particularly as Satan finds it necessary to make use of recent developments in the technology of vision from the mount, making reference to both an "optick glass" and an "aerie microscope"; Milton adding to his description of the scene from the summit: "By what strange parallax, or optic skill/Of vision, multiplied

through air, or glass/Of telescope, were curious to enquire.")

Just four years after Milton completed his epic masterpiece the theologian Thomas Burnet made the Grand Tour with the young Earl of Wiltshire, passing over the Alps on their way to Italy. He was both impressed and appalled by what he saw – "vast undigested heaps of stone" – and decided to write a book in order that he might explain how such things could have come about in God's world: "I was not easy till I could give my self some tolerable Account how that confusion came in Nature." The book, originally published in Latin as *Telluris Theoria Sacra* in 1681, before being translated, and somewhat enlarged and rewritten as *The Sacred Theory of the Earth* in 1684, disputed the biblical orthodoxy that the earth had always looked the same, or indeed, that such terrible features upon the face of the earth could hardly have been part of God's original design. Instead, Burnet proposed that the mountains were formed from the chaos of the Flood, when the rock and earth of the planet's crust was broken and swirled with devastating force before being left in terrible heaps by the receding waters. Where there had once been, before the deluge, "a wide and endless Plain, smooth as a calm sea," were now to be found "wild, vast and indigested Heaps of Stone and Earth," the most spectacular "Ruins of a broken World." We are inhabitants, in Burnet's phrase, of "a World lying in its rubbish."

Stephen Jay Gould has suggested that Burnet's book, which became known simply as 'the Theory', was the most widely-read work of geology in the 17th century, and its influence was extraordinary, although it was within aesthetics, rather than geology or theology, that its influence was perhaps felt most strongly. Despite his moral and theological revulsion of the mountains, the chaotic debris of a vengeful God, and the offence they caused his aesthetic sensibilities – "The Mountains are plac'd in no Order one with another, that can either respect Use or Beauty" – Burnet could not repress his fascination with these forms. Indeed, the chapter in which he condemns the most forcefully the gross irregularity of mountains (from which the above quotation was taken) actually begins with an acknowledgement of their magnificence:

> The greatest Objects of Nature are, methinks, the most pleasing to behold; and next to the Great Concave of the Heavens, and those boundless Regions where the Stars inhabit, there is nothing that I look upon with more pleasure than the wide Sea and the Mountains of the Earth. There is something august and stately in the Air of these things, that inspires the Mind with great Thoughts and Passions; we do naturally, upon such Occasions, think of God and his Greatness: And whatsoever hath but the Shadow and appearance of INFINITE, as all Things have that are too big for our Comprehension, they fill and overbear the Mind with their Excess, and cast it into a pleasing kind of Stupor and Admiration.

Here, for perhaps the first time in England, are presented the competing emotional claims of the *beautiful* and the *sublime*, the tension between which would inspire artists and writers for centuries to come. Wordsworth transcribed Burnet's Latin to be published with his own notes, while in Coleridge's Note Book in the British Library are to be found numerous references to the theologian, including the following proposal: "Burnet's *theoria telluris* translated into Blank Verse, the original at the bottom of the page."

There lies one-hundred-and-thirty-years between the publication of the *Sacred Theory* and Wordsworth's reading of it after his completion of *The Excursion* in 1814, however, and a certain amount of intellectual work had first to be undertaken for Burnet's publication to become a primary inspiration for the English Romantics, and, in turn, our own contrary relationship to wild nature. Even as late as 1791 the writer William Gilpin was able to declare that 'the generality of people' found wilderness disagreeable, adding that "There are few who do not prefer the busy scenes of cultivation to the greatest of nature's rough productions." Gilpin is an important figure here as it was through a number of his publications, detailing his travels in north Wales, the Scottish Highlands, and the Lake District in the latter part of the 18th century, that he attempted to establish the Picturesque as an important aesthetic category. In his classic study on the subject, the art historian Christopher Hussey remarked that "the picturesque interregnum between classic and romantic art was necessary in order to enable the imagination to form the habit of feeling through the eyes," adding that "it occurred at the point when an art shifted its appeal from the reason to the imagination." It is certainly true that before this time reference would often be made to art while attempting to describe an experience of the natural world: Malcolm Andrews describes a literary education as "an extra, expensive piece of intellectual equipment to take into the field." During their journey over the Alps in 1739, Thomas Gray was frequently reminded of passages from Livy, whilst Horace Walpole could only exclaim within a letter, "Precipices, mountains, torrents, wolves, rumblings, Salvator Rosa," the reference here painterly rather than literary, although the impulse a comparable one. Indeed, even earlier than this, in 1712, Joseph Addison could write in *The Spectator* that "We find the Works of Nature still more pleasant, the more the resemble those of Art." Yet it was with the development of the Picturesque that natural scenery came to be experience, and even judged, by the conventions of pictorial representation.

Gilpin's guide books, and those such as Thomas West's *Guide to the Lakes* (1778), were instructions not only in *what* to look at, but also *how* to look at it. In 1829 George W. Johnson remarked of Gilpin's Picturesque observations that, "If it is too much to say they formed the national taste, they served most effectually to correct it." West's *Guide*, which institutionalised the Picturesque tour of the region, was intended most explicitly for those who practice the 'noble art' of landscape painting, and led those creative tourists to a number of specific viewpoints or 'stations', which had been

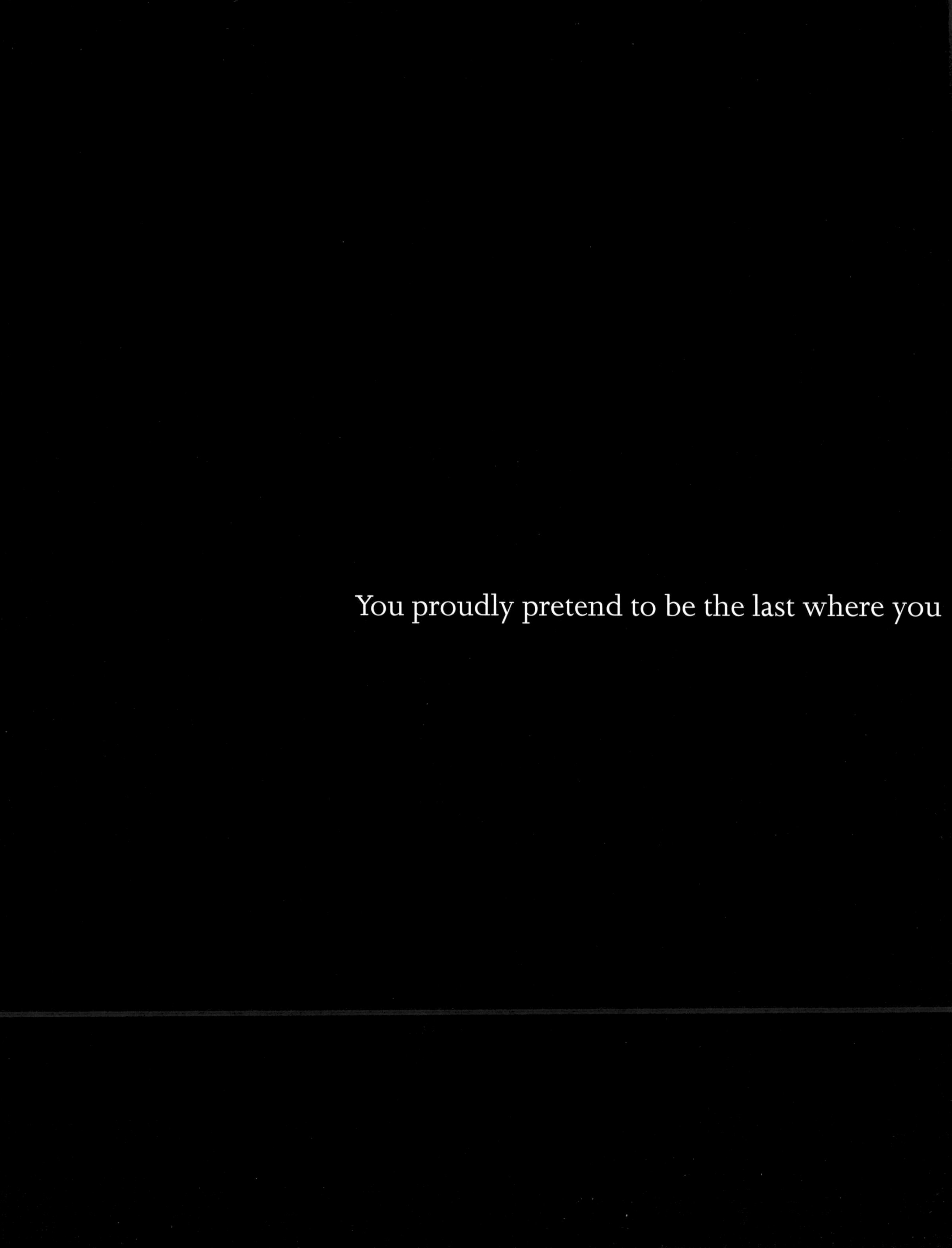

You proudly pretend to be the last where you

were once led to believe you were the first.

recommended by earlier travellers, such as Thomas Gray and Dr. John Brown. West's instructions were precise, with exact instructions as to the viewers proximity to 'two small oak trees', for example, or precisely which rock on which to stand, thereby rendering the experience of the landscape as a succession of discontinuous stops where the view most closely resembled those of a landscape painting, thus presaging the Kodak-sponsored photo-points to be found in many tourist destinations in the United States. Interestingly, many of the proposed views were not to be viewed directly, but rather reflected in a 'Claude Glass', an optical device, often consisting of a darkly-tinted small convex mirror, and bound like a pocket-book. Indeed, the view across Lake Windermere which subsequently became West's first *Station*, was already well-known at the time of Gray's visit in 1769, and the poet blindfolded himself for the ferry journey across the lake from Bowness, in order that his first sight would be that reflected upon his 'Glass'. Gilpin, too, found the device of great use, describing the view from his moving carriage thus: "A succession of high-coloured pictures is continually gliding before the eye. They are like the visions of the imagination; or the brilliant landscapes of a dream. Forms, and colours, in brightest array, fleet before us; and if the transient glance of a good composition happens to unite with them, we should give any price to fix, and appropriate the scene." (Another premonition of the photographic.)

Such a premonition perhaps suggests that we return our attention briefly to that which has prompted these historical wanderings. Indeed, wandering is precisely what is not to be found in Hugonnier's film, just as it was not in Gilpin's observations from his travelling *chaise*. Both the travelling shots from the front of the moving car, which open and close the film, and those from the drifting balloon, are far less connected to the landscape than those which are taken from a still point within the park itself. As the historian Eric Leed has noted, the traveller moves through a 'perceptual envelope', the shape of which changes according to

the speed of travel (the envelope "elongates into a tunnel as the speed of passage increases"); to the variable of speed one might also add, with reference to the balloon: the distance from the landscape across which one is travelling. Such is just one of the contradictions of an increasingly commercialised tourist industry: that in providing physical access to a particular place, that place is often made perceptually inaccessible. In diminishing the perceived particularities of place in this way, it becomes easier to diminish place in actual ways. The increased popularity of travel to the Lakes, encouraged by the guidebooks and the newly-established tours offered by Thomas Cook, led to the proposed extension of the railway line from Kendal to Windermere, something fiercely opposed by local residents. Nature would not be enough for the tourist masses, and commercial entertainments would soon be required. As Wordsworth described the concerns of the locals in the opening lines of his sonnet *On the Proposed Kendal and Windermere Railway* (1844): "Is there no nook of English country secure / From rash assault?"

Of course, the irony here is that Wordsworth was himself somewhat responsible for the growing popularity of tourism to the Lakes, following his own *Guide to the Lakes*, first published as an anonymous introduction to Joseph Wilkinson's *Select Views of Cumberland* in 1810. Such is a contradiction one must find in any consideration of tourism: that it cannot help but destroy that which it sets out to celebrate. Tributes are transformed into laments. There are certainly issues of class here, as the leisured Gentleman (and Lady) traveller of the 18th and early 19th centuries is later joined by the mass populace from whom they had perhaps been attempting to escape. Such a rise in tourist numbers necessitated travelling further afield, and having had their sensibilities heightened upon the hills of north Wales, the Lakes, and the Scottish Highlands, the leisured traveller found their way to the Alps. Such isolation was short-lived, however, and the reports of mountain ascents – both heroic and tragic – and the descriptions of what could now be

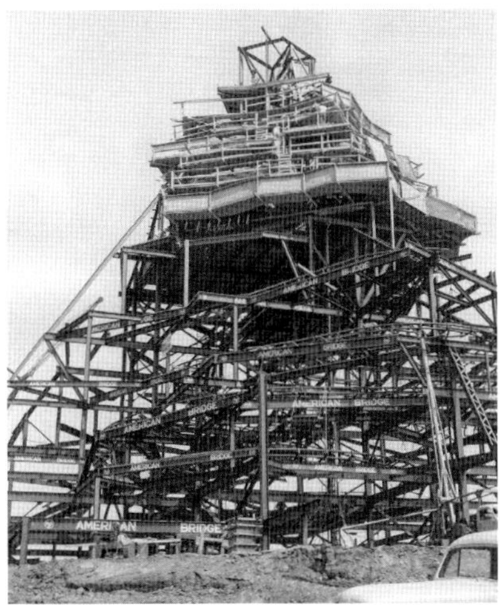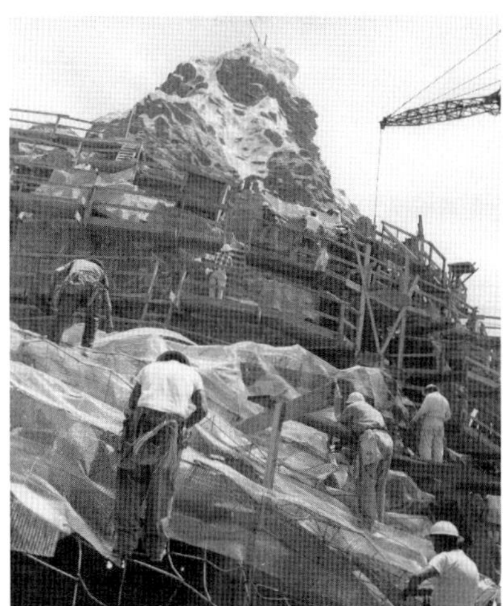

Anonymous, Construction of the Matterhorn, Disneyland,
Los Angeles 1950

appreciated as *sublime* natural scenery, soon brought tourists flocking to the region. The Alps were brought home also, in a series of public displays which celebrated the mountains, such as the large dioramas displayed in Leicester Square by Robert Burford, who advertised the show by parking his miniature plaster and papier-mâché Mont Blanc on a wagon in Oxford Street (and this over a century before Disney was to build its own synthetic paean to sublimity with a concrete Matterhorn in California). Such displays prompted the English showman Albert Smith to increase substantially his own 'Alps in a box' that he toured around the Home Counties, and in exploiting the publicity that surrounded that year's Great Exhibition, in 1851 he scaled Mont Blanc, before descending, clinging to the back of a partner, as a form of human toboggan. Just seven months later, in March 1852, 'The Ascent of Mont Blanc' opened at the Egyptian Hall in Piccadilly, London, with a pasteboard Swiss chalet, rolling dioramas, specially-composed music, such as the Chamonix Polka and the Mont Blanc Quadrille, and even a pair of chamois and St. Bernard dogs. The sublime had been transformed into showmanship.

When, in 1865, Thomas Cook extended its range of mountain tours from Britain to the Alps, the influx of tourists had the effect of turning small agricultural villages – that had often struggled to survive the lean winter months – into resort towns. New chalets and hotels were built to accommodate the growing numbers, to the despair of those who considered the region their own, a region where they could, in the words of Leslie Stephens, the president of the recently established Alpine Club, "breathe air that has not passed through a million pairs of lungs." All that could be hoped for was an act of containment: that the "kings, cockneys, persons travelling with couriers, Americans doing Europe against time … commercial travellers and especially that variety of English clergyman which travels in dazzling white ties and forces services upon you by violence in remote country inns" might be confined to places like St. Moritz "to amuse or annoy one another", just as Chamonix and

the Valais had been left to the 'tourist swarm'. It was in Chamonix in 1863 that perhaps the English language's greatest writer upon mountains, John Ruskin, bought a piece of land on which he hoped to build a house, abandoning his plans once he perceived "what ruin was inevitable in the valley after it became a tourist rendezvous." The irony is, once more, unacknowledged. Ruskin did not simply reserve his articulate, if self-righteous, fury for the tourists, however; even the mountaineers of the Alpine Club, of which he was a member, and which shared his distaste for the vulgarians such as Smith, were subject to a particularly stinging attack in a lecture delivered in 1864:

> You have despised nature; that is to say, all the deep and sacred sensations of natural scenery. The French revolutionists made stables of the cathedrals of France; you have made racecourses of the cathedrals of the earth. Your *one* conception of pleasure is to drive in railroad carriages round their aisles, and eat off their altars. You have put a railroad bridge over the falls of Schaffhausen. You have tunnelled the cliffs of Lucerne by Tell's chapel; you have destroyed the Clarens shore of the Lake of Geneva… The Alps themselves, which your own poets used to love so reverently, you look upon as soaped poles in a bear-garden, which you set yourselves to climb, and slide down again, with 'shrieks of delight'. When you are past shrieking, having no human articulate voice to say you are glad with, you fill the quietude of the valleys with gunpowder blasts, and rush home, red with cutaneous eruption of conceit, and voluble with convulsive hiccoughs of self-satisfaction.

The impact of tourism upon the landscape was the same, whether in the Alps or the Lake District. Indeed, Wordsworth makes the connection explicit in a letter to the editor of the *Morning Post* in 1844 protesting the extension of the railway line to Windermere discussed earlier. After quoting his own lines on the Simplon Pass,

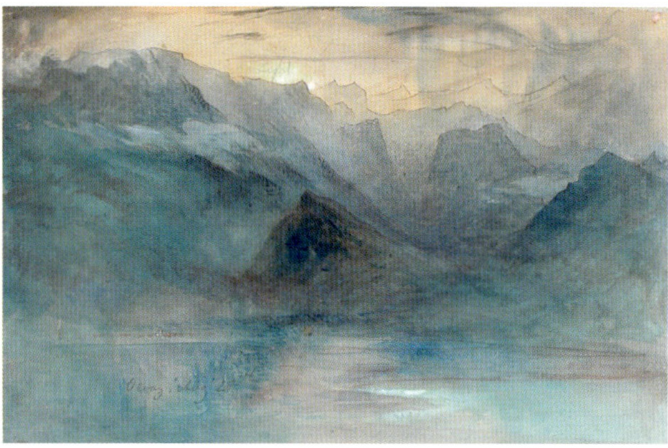

Vevey – sunrise, watercolour, heightened with white, by John Ruskin
Bequeathed to Alpine Club by C.M. Warren
© Alpine Club Photo Library, London

composed after crossing it on foot with a college friend in 1790,
Wordsworth makes reference to a more recent visit there:

> Thirty years afterwards, I crossed the Alps by the same Pass;
> and what had become of the forms and powers to which I had
> been indebted for those emotions. Many of them remained
> of course undestroyed and indestructible. But, though the
> road and torrent continued to run parallel to each other, their
> fellowship was put to an end. The stream had dwindled into
> comparative insignificance, so much had Art interfered with
> and taken the lead of Nature… The oratories heretofore not
> infrequently met with, on a road still somewhat perilous, were
> gone; the simple and rude bridges, swept away; and instead
> of travellers proceeding, with leisure to observe and feel, were
> pilgrims of fashion hurried along in their carriages, not a few
> of them perhaps discussing the merits of 'the last new novel',
> or poring over their Guide-books, or fast asleep.

Perhaps their minds were drifting, as ours might now, back to the
traveller in the back of Hugonnier's car, whose mind drifts also. The
passenger's mind is not one that seems unduly troubled with the
concerns described above; indeed, in the margins of a book she lent
me (with the appropriate title of *The Accelerated Sublime*) Hugonnier
has written: "There is nothing more that I like than being in a train
or in a plane early in the morning. To be at speed in a landscape.
It feels like you are going faster than time, faster than the day before
it happens." A viewer of this film may find reference made to the
Romantic Sublime – as Wordsworth had it so long ago, "A stranger
to mountain imagery naturally on his first arrival looks out for
sublimity in every object that admits of it" – yet in many ways it is
a more knowing work, aware of the iconography and desires of that
period whilst being careful not to fall into the conceptual crevices
that are opened by their internal tensions. If in the collection of her
thoughts published as *Gravity and Grace* we find Simone Weil's desire,

"To see a landscape as it is when I'm not there," then in *The Last Tour*
such a desire is questioned: "You are wondering about what the
park will be like when it closes. / What you foresee is what you
know from the past, / but your approach is to follow the footprints
of the near future without nostalgia. / Can you relate to the closure
of the park at all, / when everything is accessible in the world you
live in?" When this 'New World' is imagined (the very phrase
echoes with the naivety of Miranda and the cynicism of Huxley)
the animals go about their acts of attack and escape, before the
scene is superimposed by their cartoon representations at
Disneyland, dancing Christmas reindeer nodding their heads in
acknowledgement of their wild cousins, who return the gesture,
before a golden carriage makes its way in a parade before the
shrunken Matterhorn. For Bakhtin, the carnival could be considered
'life turned inside out', and therefore conceptually linked to the
menippea, a form of satire which has appeared throughout history,
from ancient Christian to Reformation writings. From Petronius'
Satyricon to Lucian's *Strange Story*, the *menippea* was a genre that moved
easily between different worlds and different times, and in which
the demands of historical realism, or even probability, were
neglected in favour of hallucination and the extraordinary. Such is
the case here also; in attempting to imagine what this place might
become once we have left it, we can only imagine it as the faint
reflection of that which we have created elsewhere, itself a faint
reflection of the originating place.

But where does this leave us? Lost, our dreams polluted?
In a somewhat obtuse political article 'The Power Void in Italy'
published in *Corriere della sera* on 1 February 1975, the writer and
film director Pier Paolo Pasolini attacks the polluted political
environment in Italy, and in particular that of the ruling Christian-
Democrats, by making reference to the 'disappearance of the
fireflies' through the pollution of the natural environment.
Pasolini, who modelled himself an outsider in the wilderness
(his collection was called *Scritti Corsari*, 'Pirate Writings', much

as Rosa modelled himself as one of the *banditti*), was not particularly
optimistic that such a poisoned atmosphere might be made more
hospitable to the fireflies, and all that they represent, although
pessimism only intensifies what hope remains. As he concludes,
in reference to Italy's state-owned electricity company, "I would
give the entire Montedison, even though it be a multinational
company, for a firefly." It is this article that has inspired the short
epilogue to *The Last Tour*, although Hugonnier's hope is carried by
a more optimistic vision. "By the end of the 20th century fireflies
had disappeared in Europe./Ideologies as a way of commitment,
as well./Lately, fireflies have been seen around the park again."
If the fireflies have returned, and with them a form of progressive
social philosophy, then we have not been abandoned in the
wilderness. Indeed, perhaps the wilderness might provide a guide
through our own moral desert as it did for Ruskin, who conceived
of his reformist St. George's Guild whilst travelling through the
Alps in 1849. In allowing such a possibility, Hugonnier's film
might be considered a poetic exploration of a task that appears
both impossible and imperative, viz., in the words of the ecologist
Aldo Leopold, "To think like a mountain."

Jeremy Millar is an artist and a curator living in Whitstable, England.

Further Reading
Malcolm Andrews, *The Search for the Picturesque* (Stanford: Stanford University Press,
1989)
Mikhail Bakhtin, *Problems of Dostoevsky's Poetics* (University of Minnesota Press, 1984)
Edward S. Casey, *Getting Back into Place — Towards a Renewed Understanding of the Place-world*
(Bloomington and Indianapolis: Indiana University Press, 1993)
Verena Andermatt Conley, *Ecopolitics — The Environment in Poststructuralist Thought*
(London and New York: Routledge, 1997)
Tim Hilton, *John Ruskin — The Early Years* (New Haven and London: Yale University
Press, 2000)
Rosemary Jackson, *Fantasy — The Literature of Subversion* (London and New York:
Methuen, 1981)
Edward King, *Sublime Inspiration* (Kendal: Abbot Hall Art Gallery, 1997)
Robert MacFarlane, *Mountains of the Mind — A History of a Fascination* (London: Granta
Books, 2004)
John Muir, *The Wilderness Journeys* (Edinburgh: Canongate, 1996)
Marjorie Hope Nicolson, *Mountain Gloom and Mountain Glory — The Development of the
Aesthetics of the Infinite* (Seattle and London: University of Washington Press,
1997)
Max Oelschlaeger, *The Idea of Wilderness* (New Haven and London: Yale University
Press, 1991)
Stephen Oettermann, *The Panorama — History of a Mass Medium* (New York: Zone
Books, 1997)
John Ruskin, *Modern Painters* (London et alia: Thomas Nelson and Sons Ltd, n.d.)
John Ruskin, *Selected Writings* ed. Kenneth Clark (London: Penguin Books, 1991)
Simon Schama, *Landscape and Memory* (London, Harper Collins, 1995)
John Urry, *The Tourist Gaze* (London et alia: Sage Publications, 2002)

Color of a Memory (Pittsburgh, USA, 1972)

2001
series of 25 posters
Offset print, photograph
59.5 x 65,8 cm

Since World War II, we have all used the same mass-produced colour film to capture the cherished moments of our lives. When we look at photographs taken in the 1970s, we can see that they have a peculiar orange tinge which is the result of a specific colour balance. Later in the 1980s, there is a redder tinge and, in the 1990s, a shift to more of a blue. In fact, the orange haze effect in the 1970s photographs is not only due to the process used; the development paper and the fact that they are now ageing, but also is the result of a marketing decision taken to match the aspirations of the moment, to represent the spirit of the time. The picture shown in this work was taken by the artist 's father in Pittsburgh, where she grew up. The reverse of the poster is an offset orange corresponding to the colour balance of a 35mm Kodachrome 100 Asa from 1972.

Shoot Photograph made by the artist's father from Mount Washington, Pittsburgh, 1972
Camera not remembered
Stock Kodachrome 100 Asa 1972
Processed not remembered
Print Ruckert, Paris
Paper Cotton Wove 350 g
Production Galerie Yvon Lambert, Paris

Reproduction 300 dpi scan from original transparency printed offset litho on Hello matt 170 gms

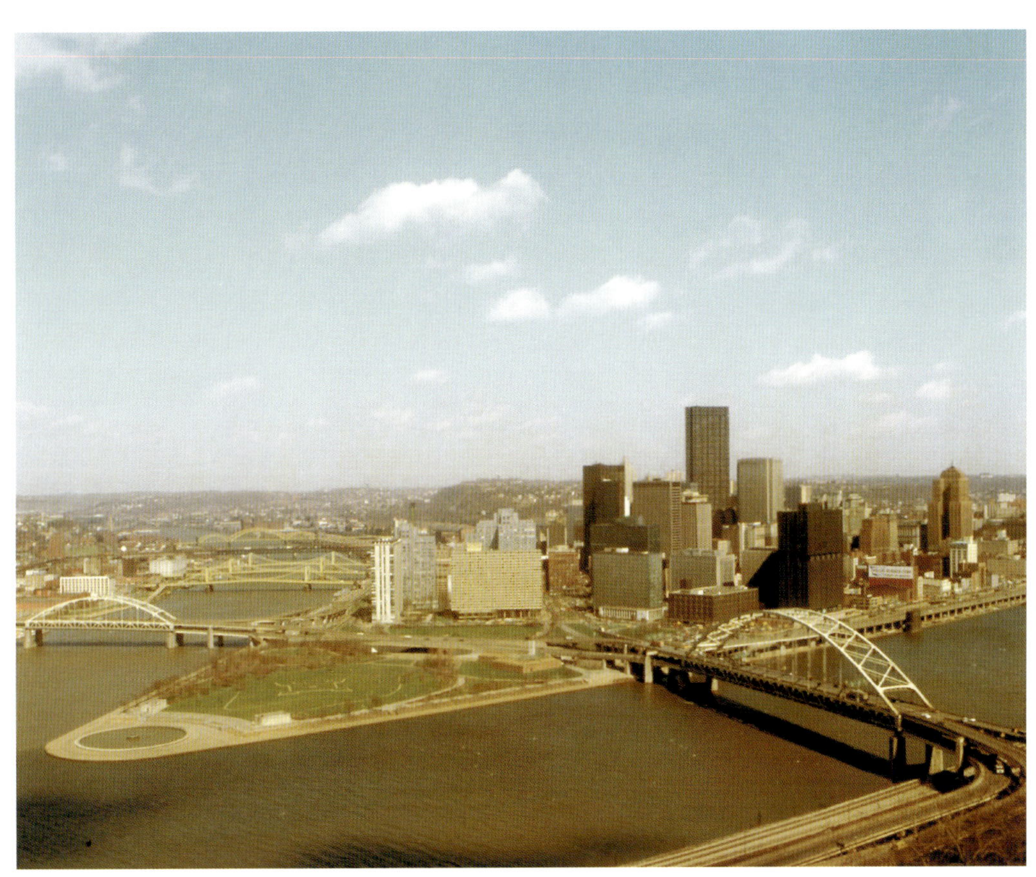

Lynne Cooke Marine, what was the basis on which this particular group of works was brought together?

Marine Hugonnier The show at DCA is a selection of works made over three years, when I was living in London. Most of the work I produced during that time had to do with how 'landscape' is a social construct; how it shapes and informs history, how it influences the course of events. Since the 19th century we have managed to create modes of analysis and perception — tools like photography and cinema — that echoed the expansionist mission of the time; that helped to establish a particular ideological and perceptual 'point of view'.

I see landscape as a form of cultural mediation. I studied anthropology and am always interested in politics and social behaviour. I spent quite a bit of time in Morocco during my childhood. One thing I remember vividly is seeing the mosaic patterns that cover the bottoms of walls at eye-level. I got used to looking at them. These abstract patterns provoked a whole world of fantasy. Because of this, I understand abstraction as an instrument of awareness: and far from a *denial* of representation. For me, that sensation was truly formative: it keeps coming into the work I make. The films and the photographs in the exhibition are about applying a kind of restriction on images, resisting the urge to add more to the world. Using images sparingly allows me to think about their status.

LC I'm left with a question of how, today, ideologies that have become extinct or disappeared (like Pasolini's elusive fireflies to which the last sequence of *The Last Tour* pays homage) might also gradually re-emerge. What might be the mechanisms, or means, by which this could happen? Through the power of love? The lure of beauty? Or flights of fantasy of the kind you experienced as a child fascinated by the patterns in mosaic tiles? If so, is this a form of romanticism?

MH I just came back from the Ramallah Film Festival in Palestine, where I saw a film projected on the notorious security wall. The film was about the construction of that wall. It reminded me of a piece by Robert Morris called *Box with the sound of its own making*, made in 1961. After that, I drove to the Dead Sea and through part of the Negev Desert thinking about your question. In the desert I stayed one night in Dimona, a brand new city built to host the labour force of the Israeli nuclear plant nearby. There I found a community of black Jews who had left Louisiana and Florida in 1969. They offered us shelter for the night. They live in the outskirts of this strange desert town. Their prefabricated houses are covered with tarpaulin, the same fabric that you find in every refugee camp. They have everything a community needs: schools, a spiritual leader, nurseries, doctors, a little hospital… As most of them are skilled carpenters and builders, they participated in the construction of Dimona, which is to say that they contributed to building Israel's military defence.

That earned them the right to stay as 'stateless' people. But, whatever their actual situation is, it made me realise that I've never had the feeling of being part of a community. If a community defines itself, or forms its identity, through its rituals and a set of common ideas, then I've simply never experienced that feeling. Except when I have found myself in the middle of a protest or demonstration. You might say that a sense of national identity can provide a feeling of belonging to a community, but I would answer: no, it does not. I guess I long for that feeling of belonging to a community.

At the end of *The Last Tour* the crew releases fireflies next to the park. For a couple of minutes, the crew forms a brief, ephemeral community. That sequence is filmed like a documentary. It stands against the first part of the film, which is fiction. There is the implication that the closure of the park, with its disavowal of spectacle and its restoring of a blank space to the map, will not only see a revival of the fireflies but also of a wider spirit of community. I didn't quite intend the crew to make such a statement. But the mechanisms or means by which ideologies might re-emerge certainly starts with constructing communities.

Both *The Last Tour* and *Towards Tomorrow (International Date Line, Alaska)* evoke particular references to Romanticism. But these works are also looking forwards; trying to define how that experience has been influenced by the techniques of the end of the 20th century, trying to define what this new feeling is. But I don't think Romanticism itself recurs in my work. *Ariana*, for example, makes more reference to history of cinema through the phenomenon of the panorama and *Flower* to *vanitas* paintings.

LC Among the key motifs usually associated with the Romantic Movement are mountains and the wilderness. Are you consciously evoking a set of references connected to that imagery and, in particular, their relation to the sublime, or are the origins of tourism, in leisure travel, more relevant here?

MH *The Last Tour* draws on representations of our relationship to landscape, and in particular, mountains, since the time when mountaineering became recognised as an activity in its own right, as something to do. It's a very short history that only started in 1787 when Horace-Bénédict de Saussure climbed up Mont Blanc in Chamonix, France.

Travel is still associated with the sublime. Since the middle ages, through the 16th century (the era of the 'Discoveries' of the so-called New World) until the beginning of the 18th century, wilderness and the feeling of the sublime inspired awe, reverence and fear. The wilderness was not a place to be; mountains were seen as accidental eyesores; and the sublime was a negative experience, as the mind was both repelled and attracted. Later, with Romanticism – and interestingly, in parallel with both the industrial revolution and a period of colonial expansionism – such Mythologies were reinterpreted. The idea of the sublime shifted and a new relationship with Nature emerged. Nature generally,

and the wilderness specifically, had an exalting and uplifting effect, was a place where one could enjoy solitary contemplation, find spiritual renewal, even something transcendent. Awe, fear, delight and rapture – all things that had previously been reserved for God – could now be expressed in one's engagement with wild nature. These two very different interpretations of the Sublime and of Nature have melded nowadays to form the language of tourism promoters.

While making *The Last Tour* I went to the Alpine Club in London to look very closely at how mountains had been represented in art. The film makes reference in many ways to mountain iconography. Painters such as Caspar Wolf, Eugène Violet Le Duc, J.M.W. Turner, Gabriel Loppe and Caspar David Friedrich chose to represent mountains through crevasses, passages, caverns and grottoes and waterfalls in the early hours of a morning or during storms. I also looked carefully at Ferdinand Hodler and Gustave Dore and the similarity in their work to the idea of 'the Fall', which is evoked at end of the film when the hot air balloon crashes.

I also was travelling through America and went to the Grand Canyon, where I soon realised that I was usually being led to a number of designated viewpoints, picturesque 'vistas' that were increasingly reducing the landscape to a series of 'spots to stop'. The landscape was fragmented like a sequence. Standing at these viewpoints, I was able to map the image I had previously had of the place onto what I was actually seeing there and then. In other words, I could test the accuracy of the encoded image I already had in my brain. I had also came across a book at the Alpine Club in London which raised the possibility of these parks coming to a complete closure. The idea of package holidays promoting a 'last tour' came across as a good starting point for a film. And I thought that this point of closure could in some way symbolise the end of the age of spectacle. *The Last Tour* is a little science fiction essay, a lyrical piece, a fantasy as opposed to *Ariana*, which is more of a documentary.

The film tries to update the feeling we have of geography

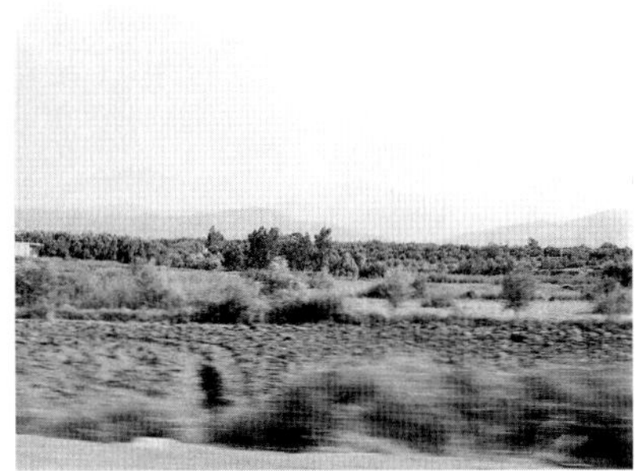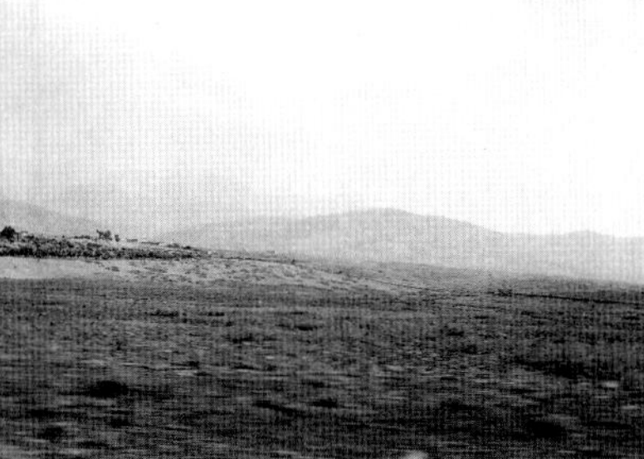

Untitled, polaroids, Marine Hugonnier, 2004
part of an ongoing series made by the artist

nowadays. Geography used to have to do with measuring space: today it seems to be linked to time. We could call it a 'geography of time', which is influenced by speed. High-speed travel has affected the way I relate to landscape and nature. I've always preferred to travel very early in the morning; what I like best is to take the Eurostar and go through the landscape at great speed as the sun rises. It feels as if I am going faster than the day to come.

When, in *The Last Tour*, the 'new world' sequence starts, you see wild animals and you hear strange noises, but overlapping these you also see images from Walt Disney — the Disney Parade and the fake Matterhorn from Disneyland, in Los Angeles.

The Last Tour is in some way addressed to a kid who happens to think that the forest that he is walking through smells like IKEA. He experiences a representation of the natural world before he actually goes there. A synthetic experience now precedes the real thing. It's more true perhaps for a younger generation than it is for mine, but there is no nostalgia in the film. I do not know what the landscape looks like when I am not there, but I do know that the body of received images that I have in my mind creates my idea of the landscape and this conditions the experience I have when I am there.

LC I like very much your analogy of the child for whom the IKEA experience and confrontation with nature in its 'raw state' are somehow equivalent, one no better or worse than the other, both interesting in their respective and interchangeable ways. The issue seems, however, that the park could be closed permanently (whether due to environmental or ecological reasons, not to mention terrorism and warfare). Must it take a new crisis to engender new ideals and goals? Don't we already have a sufficiently extreme state of crisis?

MH I guess it takes a new crisis to hear and admit that new ideals can be viable alternatives. These new ideals are here in seed form, it just takes the right set of circumstances for them to arise. Our present contains traces of that future, for sure. I guess we would all want our work, whether it is art or not, to be able to engender action but it very rarely penetrates a broader social sphere, affecting social behaviour and therefore politics. I would trust and hope that an event like the Ramallah Film Festival that gets people and ideas together would, however, have some influence over the situation.

LC Is *The Last Tour* really lyrical, as you say, or, rather, isn't it elegiac? If so, is the problem then how to engender wonder rather than melancholy and lament? How to provoke action instead of rumination? And how to encourage communal over cellular growth? Alternatively, do we sometimes need lyricism and fantasy as necessary forms of escape or solace?

MH *The Last Tour* is not elegiac. Like you I quite like that kid who wears a hood and had confused IKEA and a forest. The melancholy of the first part of the film, the fictional part of it, which might be also that kid's melancholy, doesn't imply social inaction. The fireflies at the end of the film are there to prove so.

LC What kind of work you want to make now? Do you want to follow both of the modes you have used to date: the quasi-documentary and the sci-fi fantasy?

MH I'd like to keep on making films, including more 'quasi-documentaries', as you say — there is some aspect of reality shown which doesn't appear to be documentary but yet isn't quite fiction. Fiction is to me quite melancholic, it is an altered reality. Fiction makes reality look not so well adjusted. But Truth should appear right in between these two genres.

A few years ago I made three little films with scenes I captured on the street. Their titles are simply the names of the places and the times when each scene happened. I would like to go back to that, and choose places and moments which are interesting in relation to their cultural and geographical contexts. I quite like those 'interludes' on Euro News called 'No Comment', which are images illustrating the headlines without any commentary. I may go to both Iran and Cuba soon. If I do I'll carry a 16mm camera with me. I don't yet have a project. I'll start by wondering.

LC   What you say brings this quote from Toni Negri to mind. It's from his letter to Nanni, on Construction (Arte y Multitudo, 1988): '..*The possibility of constructing the world lies entirely within our hands. To construct it, just as it has been possible for us to deconstruct it. In this radical operation, art foreruns the global movement of humanity.... In other words, making something beautiful is necessarily revolutionary.*' Does this resonate for you?

MH   I quite like this quote of Toni Negri. He uses the word 'operation' and I think that art should operate, affect reality, put issues into crisis. That may sound idealistic but I will stick to it. It doesn't mean that it has any effect on real politics. I don't know if beauty is revolutionary though. I can understand that sentence if the word 'beauty' is taken to mean 'the expression of a free will'.

I haven't lived through any revolutions, though my parents did. They met on the barricades in Paris during May '68. They were 17 and 21. I grew up with this glow of Utopia running through the house. Toni Negri was an important figure, the Red Brigade's issues were discussed. My parents were leftist and very active politically. They made us aware very early on. Political commitment was vital.

There is one thing I know of which is truly revolutionary – apart from Rock'n Roll – and that's love. As Toni Negri would say, love constructs a community of knowledge and desire. Love has to become constitutive of the 'other'. Love is an essential key: it transforms what is your own into something communal. That's a very materialist description of love, but if you apply this to reality it actually works, and quite nicely.

Lynne Cooke has been a curator at the DIA Art Foundation in New York since 1991, and is a writer on contemporary arts.

SOLO EXHIBITIONS

2004   *The Last Tour*, Magazino d'Arte Moderna, Rome
        Marine Hugonnier, Dundee Contemporary Arts, Dundee
        The Last Tour, Ariana, Kunstwerke, Berlin
        The Last Tour, Galerie Judin Belot, Zürich

2003   *Marine Hugonnier*, Galerie Yvon Lambert, Paris
        Ariana, Spacex Gallery, Exeter
        Ariana, Chisenhale Gallery, London
        Ariana, MW Projects, London
        Impact, Yokohama Red Brick Warehouse Number 1, Yokohama

2002   *Anna Hanusova. 27.06.01, 5:4"*, Trans space, New York
        Towards Tomorrow, MW Projects, London

2001   *Anna Hanusova. 27.06.01, 5:4"*, Annet Gelink Gallery, Amsterdam
        Centro Galego de Arte Contemporanea, Santiago de Compostela *
        Anna Hanusova. 27.06.01, 5:4", Kerstin Engholm Gallery, Vienna

2000   *Interlude*, Galerie Chantal Crousel, Paris *
        Fig-1, London *
        Art Unlimited, Basel

* indicates publication

GROUP EXHIBITIONS

2004   *Utopia Station*, curated by Molly Nesbit, Hans-Ulrich Obrist and
        Rirkrit Tiravanija, Mostra d'oltre Mare, Naples
        Neue Gesellschaft für Bildende Kunst (NGBK), Berlin
        Attitudini, curated by Lorenzo Buni Castel S. Pietro, Bologna
        Terratories, Malmö Kunsthall, curated by Anselm Franke
        Todo va a estar bien, Museo Tamayo Arte Contemporaneo, Mexico
        Landscape and Memory, La Casa Encendida, Madrid
        Britannia Works, British Council, curated by Katerina Gregos, Ileana
        Tounta Contemporary Art Centre, Xippas Gallery, and Breeder, Athens
        Fade In: New Film and Video, Brown Foundation Gallery of the
        Contemporary Arts Museum, Houston

2003   *Dialogues, Quand on pose une chose contre une autre, elles se touchent*, Centre
        Régional d'Art Contemporain, Sète
        Elephant Juice o sexo entre amigos, Kurimanzutto, Mexico City
        Cine y Casi Cine, curated by Berta Sichel and Pablo Llorca,
        Museo Nacional Centro d'arte Reina Sofia, Madrid
        Utopia Station, curated by Molly Nesbit, Hans-Ulrich Obrist and
        Rirkrit Tiravanija, 50th International Biennale di Venezia
        Spiritus, Magasin 3, Stockholm

2002   *Nuit Blanche*, Les Pompes funèbres, Paris
        Geographies #2, Hugonnier, Sala, Khan, Gussin, Galerie Chantal Crousel, Paris
        The Mind is a Horse, Bloomberg Space, London
        Post-VCR-Art, Tyneside Cinema, Newcastle upon Tyne
        Confiture demain..., Centre d'Art Contemporain, Sète
        Marine Hugonnier & Bernard Joïsten, FRAC Languedoc-Roussillon,
        Montpellier
        Less Ordinary, Kyungjoüo and Artsonje Centre, Seoul *
        Presentness is grace: Experiencing the present moment, Arnolfini, Bristol *
        Traversées, l'ARC, Musée d'art Moderne de la Ville de Paris, Paris *
        Unreal time video, Fine art center of KCAF, Séoul *
        Squatters, Fundaçao de Serralves, Porto *
        Beau Monde: Toward a Redeemed Cosmopolitanism, Santa Fe's Fourth
        International Biennial, New Mexico
        My Generation, Atlantis Gallery, London
        Movimientos Inmoviles, Museo de Arte Moderno, Buenos Aires *
        Marine Hugonnier & Henrik Plenge Jakobson, Centre d'Art Neuchâtel,
        Neuchâtel

2000   *Permanencia voluntaria*, Cinémania, Kurimanzutto, Mexico
        Mexico City Cinema Festival, Cinemax World Trade Center, Mexico
        Vivre sa vie, Tramway, Glasgow *

2004   *3 to the Power of 3:1*, Cine Lumière, curated by Ian White, London
2003   *Ariana, 9th Brief Encounters International Short Film Festival*, Watershed and
            IMAX Cinema, Bristol
            Ariana, 'Migrations' at Dartington, Devon
2002   *Anna Hanusova. 27.07.01 5:40"*. Soho House, London
            Anna Hanusova. 27.07.01 5,40". Stadtkino, Art Film Kunsthalle Basel
            Anna Hanusova. 27.07.01 5,40". Rotterdam Film Festival, Musée
            Boijmans-van Beuningen, Rotterdam,
2001   *Set. Racconto e artificio*, Cinema Massimo, Torino, with the collaboration
            of the Museo Nazionale del Cinema and Castello di Rivoli
            Rencontres vidéo, Galerie Française, Piazza Navona, Rome

COLLECTIONS

Musée d'art Moderne de la Ville de Paris
Fundaçao de Serralves, Porto
Centro Galego de Arte Contemporanea, Santiago de Compostela
Fonds National d'art contemporain (FNAC), Paris
Collection La Gaia, Italy
Fondation pour la MAN, Luxembourg
Thyssen-Bornemisza Contemporary Art Foundation, Vienna
Jumex Collection, Mexico

Marine Hugonnier would like to thank:

Max Wigram, Michael Briggs, Del Ruby Winter, Soraya Rodriguez, Juliette
Blightman and Alec Steadman at MW Projects, London; Juerg Judin at Galerie
Judin, Zürich; Steven Bode, Mike Jones, Caroline Smith, Nina Ernst, Bevis Bowden
and Keith Whittle at Film and Video Umbrella, London; Katrina Brown and Colin
Lindsay at Dundee Contemporary Arts, Dundee; Martine Aboucaya, Olivier Belot,
Yvon Lambert, Elodie Cazes and Muriel Quancard at Galerie Yvon Lambert,
Paris/New York; Jean Dominique Secondi, Renaud Sabari and Alexandra Cohen
at Art Public Contemporain, Paris; Palmina D'Ascoli, Aurelie Bruhl and Blanche
de Tannery at Villa Medicis hors les Murs, Paris.

Michael Newman, Lynne Cooke, Jeremy Millar, Martin Herbert, Mark Godfrey,
Daniel McClean.

Aurelien Bras, Ida Bregninge, Ami Barak, Nathalie Bertaux, Patricia Craig,
Julie and Romain Gonssard-Poucet, Fernando Gutierrez, Christian Manzutto,
Emmanuelle and Nicolas Fouks Mauriac, Sebastien Roux, Paul Stzulman,
Tom Townend,

Adam Broomberg

Families Van Burren-Hugonnier and Demoury-Hugonnier

Marine Hugonnier is represented by:
MW Projects 43b Mitchell Street, London EC1V 3QD
T: +44 (0)20 7251 3194 E: info@mwprojects.net www.mwprojects.net

Galerie Judin Lessingstrasse 5, Zürich CH 80002
T: +41 (43) 344 5561 E: judin@galeriejudin.ch www.galeriejudin.ch

Marine Hugonnier
Published by Film and Video Umbrella and Dundee Contemporary Arts
Edited by Steven Bode and Katrina M. Brown
Editorial Assistance from Nina Ernst and Anne-Marie Watson
Designed by SMITH
Printed by Dexter Graphics
© 2004 Film and Video Umbrella, Dundee Contemporary Arts,
the artist and the authors
ISBN 1 90427 012 3

Film and Video Umbrella
52 Bermondsey Street
London SE1 3UD
T: +44 (0)20 7407 7755
F: +44 (0)20 7407 7766
E: info@fvu.co.uk
www.fvumbrella.com

Dundee Contemporary Arts
152 Nethergate
Dundee DD1 4DY
T: +44 (0)1382 909900
F: +44 (0)1382 909221
E: dca@dca.org.uk
www.dca.org.uk

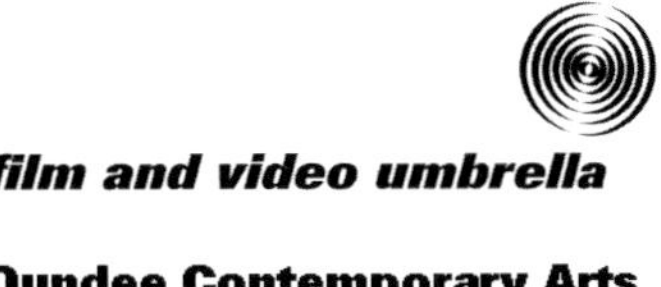
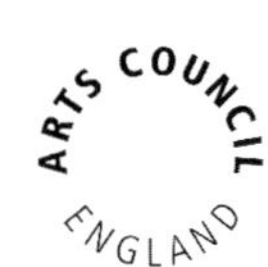
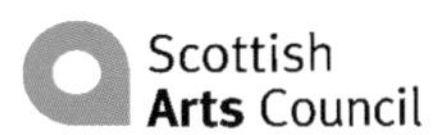
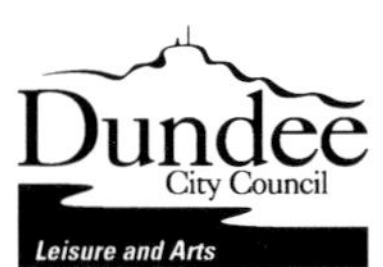